ONE LIFE
TWO CONTINENTS
TWO CULTURES

An Autobiography by
Jagir Singh Kalu

Published by BookPublishingWorld 2021

Copyright © Jagir Singh Kalu 2021

ISBN: 978-1-8384967-6-0

BookPublishingWorld
An imprint of Dolman Scott
www.dolmanscott.com

Dedication

This book is dedicated to all our Grandchildren. It is also dedicated to our grandson Emmanuel Wallis and my sister-in-law Melanie Oldacre who are no longer with us.

Note

Many of the names in this manuscript have been changed to protect identities including the Author's.

Preface

I am writing this autobiography intending to leave a legacy for my wife, children, grandchildren; and maybe great-grandchildren; of my background, and cultural heritage of my family and my life in India. They must understand their roots. I hope by reading this, they will become more tolerant and empathetic to the needs of people from all races regardless of their religion, colour, disability, or background. I hope the children will learn to put things in perspective and maybe learn from my experience for generations to come. The Indian culture has changed immensely over the past sixty years and it continues to evolve. Therefore, what seemed right at the time may not be so now. Having given further thought and encouragement by others, I decided to make it generally available for wider circulation.

As I write this, I want the readers to understand that my story began when I was a child, I understood as a child, and acted like a child. Over a while, some of the memories fade away but many have a lasting effect on your life and those all around you. As a child, you look at life from a very different perspective.

Since arriving in the UK, I have had the privilege of visiting India on several occasions and my last two visits were in April 2018 and October 2019 with some members of my family and grandchildren. My wife and I, together with some of the other grandchildren and their parents, had planned to go in April 2020. This visit had to be canceled due to the Corona virus.

In India, things are very different now, due to many changes that have taken place since the independence of India. Life was very different then, in comparison to how it is now. India has developed economically, culturally, and socially. The digital age has had a great impact on the world in which we live today, and India has contributed greatly and embraced its challenges. Family values are constantly changing and will continue to change. We also have to acknowledge that people who came to this country in the 1950s and 60s and before that, were only familiar with what was culturally and religiously practiced and acceptable at the time they left for the UK. They adhered to those values not knowing that these practices were evolving and they still are. The second consideration that needs to be borne in mind is that India had only just gained its independence from the British Empire and the displacement of millions of people during the separation between India and Pakistan was less than ten years. Democracy, social mobility, and equality are still developing and so will its impact on society, its culture, and values.

Finally, I decided to write this autobiography in two parts. The first part of this autobiography, consisting of my life as a single, unmarried person, and the second part of the autobiography, following my marriage to my ever-loving wife Brenda Dorothy Talbott in August 1974.

Madan Kallow

Index

Part 1

Part 2

Part 1

Chapter 1

The Beginning. (1953)

He had left us earlier on. I could vaguely remember, comprehend, or accept why. There he was and then he was no longer there. How long would it be this time? There was no explanation at all. I was about 5 years of age at the time. I do remember there being a lot of comings and goings and then one early morning, whilst it was still dark, I can recall the devas and the smell of paraffin lamps being lit, the clinking of the pots and pans, the whispering, and then the aroma of food being prepared. I was half asleep, rubbing my eyes and then covering myself under the Rajai (quilt) as my face felt the chill of the new morn. It was quite a frosty morning as it does get quite cool during the night. I tried to keep warm without being too intrusive or inquisitive. They tried not to make too much noise so they would not wake up the neighbours. We, the children, were in the way, as we always were. We were not important at all and ignored most of the time. They had so many things to do and to think about. I had no idea what was going on, but I was becoming very inquisitive and my mind was racing from one thing to the other. Just what is going on? I bet the neighbours knew and probably the rest of the world knew but I, not at all. I could not sleep but pretended to be. However, I do remember my maternal grandmother, Dhano Kaur standing by the door, holding a deva lamp. There was a solemn expression on her face. She was looking rather gloomy and expressionless as if her world had fallen apart. It probably had but how was I to know. Even if I knew, I could not do anything about it anyway. Her face was covered with wrinkles and her cheeks were covered in crevices and folds, which were partly reflected by the glow of the flickering flame of the divas. This could only be from the stress and worry about her family's circumstances, especially about her one and only daughter, my mother, Swaran Kaur. She had every right to worry about it. There were lots of uncertainties about what was going on. Would it work out alright or not? Would we ever see him again? Would he make it? As the activities of the early morning died down, it all went very quiet and we all went to bed again as if nothing had happened. How the rest of his journey went, I have no idea. This was the last time I saw my father until we as a family came from India to join him on 4th April 1960 on a dark and bitterly cold night. This was indeed a new beginning for us as a family into the unknown.

Chapter 2

My Paternal Family

My father, Kishan Singh Kalu was the second eldest of three brothers and one sister. He married Swaran Kaur Raju in 1936 when my mother was just 14 years of age. He was born and bred in a very small village in Soos, which we pronounced as Susa, a short distance away from Hoshiarpur city in Punjab. My memory goes back to one of our very rare family visits to this village. I must have been around seven years of age at the time. Travelling between Hoshiarpur and Susa was not just difficult, but it was virtually impossible using any mode of transport. The only public transport, a bus, travelled to the outskirts of the main outlying villages and from there we had to hire a tractor or a Tonga (horse and carriage) to the outskirts of Susa. We then rolled up the bottoms of our pyjama suits to avoid them being either wrapped or torn by various obstacles on the muddy footpath or the edges of the fields or grass reeds and barks as we walked the rest. It was even more difficult if it happened to be the rainy season. The path had been well-trodden and the barley and maize fields had been parted to make a path. This was the only way of getting to Susa. There was no tarmac road to the village or even a good mud track for the last few miles. If you wanted to get to the village, the only way to get there was to walk across the edges of numerous fields, that is if you knew the way. I remember the fields being lush and green, growing sugar cane, corn on the cob, barley and wheat, and other such crops. There was field after field yielding the harvest which had to be crisscrossed, as well as the odd stream to jump over depending upon the season. On the way to Susa, we had to go past wooded areas some containing large oak trees, walnut trees, plum trees, and others. We were quite young at the time and we were told of a naked man who lived in these woods. He was like a giant and had a long bushy grey beard and long grey matted hair. The stench heaving from his body would mark the spot. He never washed and he lived amongst the animals. At times, he would yell making deep crying distressed noises, especially during the night. He was considered demon-possessed and had no contact with the outside world. We were warned never to approach these woods because something awful would happen to us. He could kill us if we came into contact with him. As we walked past these woods, my heart would pound and beat faster and faster as if I had been running a marathon. I would be very vigilant as we walked as a family along the edges of the fields adjacent to these woods and I ensured that I stayed close with the others. I could not wait to go past these woods.

Susa, my Dad's village was quite a small and poverty-stricken village with most of the people trying to make a meager living out of farming. All they had was a bucket and a kahi, (a small spade used for digging the field). As we approached the village we could see and hear numerous dogs barking at us because we were strangers. As we approached the neighbourhood, we were greeted by a large herd of goats. As they came towards us, we tried to avoid them like the plague because we did not want to get our clothes any dirtier than they already were from walking across the fields to get to the village. Our shoes were plastered in mud and we would not be able to tell the original colour of what we were wearing. Although we were not wearing socks, we would avoid sliding from side to side in the mud to avoid further embarrassment of our already dirty clothes.

My memories of that visit are quite vivid. As I approached the house I saw few men sitting outside and I remember one of them walking past us with no top on, just a dhoti, (a loin cloth) having a long dirty, bushy, white beard, and using a lathi, which is, a long walking stick used as a support. I can still picture us approaching the house. As we got nearer, we realised my paternal grandmother and few members of her family were expecting us. They knew we had arrived because the word had spread that we were approaching the house. This is the house where my father was born and their family mud house stood on the edge of the village. I remember visiting the village about twice before coming to England. As we approached the house, we saw a very small boundary wall about three feet high which was made of mud and straw around the house. It was barely able to support itself because it was crumbling away bit by bit. They say that mud sticks, but I can assure you, this mud didn't. I was not familiar with the surroundings of the house or with any of the area. There was no one else that I knew. Being there was very strange. We were not allowed to go out by ourselves even if we wanted to. I don't even recall there being a grocery or a sweet shop but there must have been one or two. This mud house also had a small open courtyard and in it, I do remember there being a small cooking area where the chulla, (clay fire pit) stood. The floor had a covering of clay and the walls of the house were made of clay and straw. This house had two very small, dingy, dark rooms. It was like entering into a cave. It was dark inside with no outside light beaming in. It seemed very strange as you entered the rooms because you had to wait for your eyes to adjust to the darkness. Both of the rooms had a bed with linen on it.

This house was occupied by my paternal grandmother and one of my young cousins. He was about ten or eleven years of age at that time and he was the carer who looked after her. Apart from the manja (bed) and the torn dirty bed linen, the rooms were bare. I could see no other clothes or items of furniture or any personal belongings. There was nothing for us, the children, to do except to sit there and entertain ourselves. I don't remember much about the village, the people, the neighbours or any landmarks. It was boring beyond imagination and it seemed to me that time had stood still. Being there, we had no one else to interact with except our own family who was not a great deal of fun. The time in the village seemed never-ending, waiting an eternity for anything to happen. Sadly, most of the time nothing happened. There was no excitement in our lives. I can picture my paternal grandmother sitting there on a fatta, which is a small foot stool. As soon as we entered the house, all of us had to perform the usual customary cultural greetings. All of the children had to get on their hands and knees and bow down to the older members of the family. We had to touch their feet with our hands and then touch our forehead with the same hand. This was a way of showing respect to our elders. However, as children, we had to bow down to them on all four in front of them. This was quite an embarrassing and tedious chore. There was no choice or you get a reputation for stubbornness and for causing further embarrassment to the family.

I cannot recall my paternal grandmother's name or her age except that she looked as if she was getting on a bit by now. I suppose she must have been about the same age as my maternal grandmother but she looked much older and frailer. Her head was shaking all the time and she had this tremor in her hands. Of course, as children, we didn't know at the time what it was or its effects. We had no diagnosis and it is very unlikely that she would have seen a doctor about it. There were no doctors in the village and if there were, they would not have been qualified enough to diagnose this type of condition, and most of all, she would not be able to afford even the consultation never mind any medication.

My paternal grandmother later went to live in Amritsar, the home of the Golden Temple and my Chacha, my Dad's younger brother. She was there for a short time and then she went to live in Pathiana with her daughter. This is where she was living the last time I saw her but since then she has died. I had no idea of her age when she died. I last saw her in 1990 during my visit with my brother to India. I am certain that she did not know who we were. There was hardly any conversation exchanged between us either way. She looked so frail and she was shaking uncontrollably. We spent about ten minutes with her. As there was no communication between us, all we could do was to stand there and gaze at her feeling totally helpless. We had some difficulty finding her place but she was living very near the other members of her family, our cousins, whom we did not know. This was the first time that we had met our paternal cousins. We felt disheartened because our flesh and blood had no idea who we were or why had we come. She just sat there in that little dingy and dismal place, with no mental stimulation and not a great deal of interaction with the other members of her family or the community. She had several grand and great-grandchildren and maybe even great, great-grandchildren but she appeared to be a lifeless lonely figure, who was just watching and waiting but didn't know for what or when. She was in a sad state at least from our perspective. There was no daycare but just care in the community, by the immediate family who took care of her physical necessities. This was normal life for a person with that type of illness. We spent few minutes with our other cousins whom we had never seen before as it was courteous to see and spend a little with them out of duty. They were strangers to us and had no guarantee that they wanted to see us except out of curiosity and family duty. Whilst there, they took us to their house but not inside as it was a beautiful hot day. They took us to the top of the house via a set of external stairs to the flat roof top and showed us different parts of the village. After about half an hour we did our formalities, gave them a few rupees, and left as was customary. There was no customary hospitality from them to decline considering we had travelled several miles in the heat of the day to make this journey to see our paternal grandmother. On the other hand, they were not expecting us as we just dropped in on them. Hospitality was the least of our concerns. That was our last visit to Pathiana or to any other paternal members of our family. It is quite difficult to socialize when you live thousands of miles away and you only have a limited time and not a great deal in common because they are strangers to us.

Following this visit, I was fairly sure that that this would be the last time, I would see my paternal grandmother. There should have been a great deal of sadness in my heart at leaving her but although it was there, it was not immense. This is someone I do not remember a great deal, nor had much to do with. I do not remember being held by her or her being someone who took any interest in my affairs or laughed and joked with me as a young child. There was no interaction between us because we did not have regular contact with her. Even when I visited Soos, there was not a great deal of interest from her toward us. She was just a family figure who happened to be our paternal grandmother.

My Dad had two brothers, one younger and one older, as well as an older sister, and they all lived in Amritsar, the home of the Golden Temple. The younger brother was Kehar Singh Kalu. As I recall, he had an office job. He was a smart, well-dressed, and affluent man. He was of medium height and build and he would go to work on his bike as did the majority of the people in those days. He wore a deep blue turban around his head which was evenly wound and knotted. This identified him as belonging to the Sikh religion. Often he would wear a thathi (cloth) around his chin to cover his beard. He would wrap the thathi very tight and then finish off by twirling the end of his mustache like the end of a shuttle and let that stick out. This was a symbol of his power and authority. It made him look good and gave him the status that he commanded. His first wife died before I was ten years old. I don't remember her at all but I do remember his second wife. We had to call her chachee as she was the wife of my father's younger brother. She was also a widow and she had one daughter and an older son from her previous marriage. I cannot recall her name, however, I do remember visiting Amritsar on several occasions and spending few days there and enjoying her cooking.

Both my Chacha and Chachee (my father's younger brother and his wife) lived in a small compact government terrace block apartment. The accommodation just consisted of a small lounge which also doubled up as a bedroom and the rear of the apartment was open with no roof and was used as a kitchen. There were no toilets in the apartment although this was nothing unusual. The complex had a block of toilets outside which were about 30 yards away from where my uncle lived. There were two latrine blocks, one for males and the other for females with holes in the ground and a small water tap about ten inches up from the floor. The stench coming from these toilets was unbearable and continued to get worse as time went by and the temperature increased during the day. If you were a visitor, you didn't have to ask where the latrines were, you just had to follow your nose. These toilets were shared by the whole complex. Although these toilets were awful, I have been to worse ones in France whilst holidaying there.

I cannot recall the sleeping arrangements where I slept in that house but I must have done. Chachee's daughter, who I met for the first time was of similar age and did not permanently live with them in Amritsar but I do remember seeing her when she came to stay in Amritsar at the same time as I was staying. She was a lovely girl and very kind. I recall playing with her. The house had electricity which would go on and off for no apparent reason. As I mentioned earlier, our family was poor but the family in Amritsar were making a reasonable living. To keep the cost of their electricity down they would bypass the meter. The whole wiring system was in a tangle. Chacha connected additional wires to the input wires before they entered the meter to draw electricity which they would use to power their house. They had to remember to remove these wires before letting in the electric meter reader, otherwise, their misdeed would be discovered. As Chacha was out at work all day, it was Chachee's responsibility to disconnect these wires. Whilst there I do remember the meter reader man coming and Chachee didn't have time to remove these wires. I am not sure what happened about this afterward.

Chacha would visit Mum in Jandiala, our village, from time to time, and on each visit, he would come to ask for money. He thought we were well off as my father was in England and therefore, he would be making a good living which indeed was not the case. My father would send the money from the UK to Mum for the family every month and it would be just under 100 rupees. Although the money was sent to Mum it was always Mama (uncle) who would sign for it and the odd few pasas of change would be given to the postman as a tip for delivering the money. Every time Chacha came, he returned with money even if Mum had to borrow it from others and then later pay it back. Later Chacha started his own business in the textile industry. He wrote to Dad in England who sent him money on numerous occasions but it would never be enough as he always wanted more. Whatever the family circumstances were at that time, I immensely enjoyed my stay with my Chacha and Chachee. They looked after me well and I do not recall them mistreating me in any way. It was quality time. Staying with them was a happy time and I always looked forward to the next visit which was always during the school vacation.

During one of my stays in Amritsar, I must have been about ten years old at the time and it was Diwali day (Festival of Light Celebration day throughout India). This was an annual event. For some reason unknown to me, I had to return immediately home to Jandiala. I had no idea what that was about and I still don't know to this day. It was the morning and I do recall my Chacha taking me to the railway station on his bike and buying a train ticket, giving me 10 rupees to give to my Mum, and then putting me on the train. I travelled alone to Jandiala from Amritsar about sixty miles. He would have no idea if I had arrived in Jandiala or not. I had never travelled alone on a train previously. I had to change trains in Jalandhar including the platform and then catch the train to Jandiala and then get off at the local railway station. The train station was about a mile or a mile and a half from the village. I recall getting off the train and then walking home across the fields, cutting across the sugar cane fields which were much taller than I. It was quite confusing and disorientating being in the field. I aimed in the direction I wanted to go but where I ended up was completely different. I knew my way around the village, so reaching home was not a problem. On reaching home, I gave the ten rupees to Mum who was surprised at receiving the money and she was so grateful saying, she didn't have any money for food or Diwali celebrations. As evening approached, the whole village was being lit with divas. The divas were filled with rape seed oil and the wicks were made by rolling cotton wool in your hands and then placing them in the diva. You had to make sure that the wicks were immersed in oil before being lit. All these divas were placed on the window ledges, roof ledges, on the walls, and where ever you could find a space for them. There were thousands of these being lit in the village. To celebrate Diwali, we would dress in our best clothes, have nice food and eat plenty of Indian sweets. These were the highlights. Also during Diwali, I remember a small fair coming to the village consisting of small rides propelled by boys and men. The music was loud and the whole of the village would hear it, there was no escape. It was quite a novelty as we did not hear much music except on the odd occasion, which would be on special occasions such as when a wedding took place in the village, or some entertainer passing through. Hardly anybody had a radio in the village, so we had to rely on these special occasions. It was a great time for us, the children and we always looked forward to it.

My eldest paternal uncle, whom we called Thaia and his wife Thaiee, also lived in Amritsar about ten minutes walk away from my uncle Kehar Singh. His name was Mahiaa Singh Kalu but I can't remember Thaiee's name. They also occupied a government apartment which was not that big. Travelling between the two apartments was the main railway line where the trains frequently passed. On numerous occasions, while travelling between these locations with one of my cousins, we played on these railway lines. They had steam-powered trains at the time. We used to put a Pesa (penny) on the railway lines and then wait for the train to go over it. Once the train has gone over the penny, then we would try to find the penny and then see how much it had been flattened and stretched. These were nice days to remember as it brings back many happy memories. I don't remember a great deal about Thaia and Thaiee, but I think they had four children and three of them were boys. I did not have a great deal of contact with them and I only saw them when I visited Amritsar and whilst there, I always stayed with Chacha and Chachee. As a family, we did not have a great deal of contact due to the distance. Amritsar is about sixty miles away from Jandiala, so we only visited each other if there was a particular reason such as a wedding, death, etc. As far as I know, Thaia and Thaiee or any other members of their family ever coming to our village to visit us. Come to think of it, there was never any reason for my mother to visit Amritsar. Life was dull and dreary for every member of our family. Travelling costs money and none of us had it. On our first return visit to India in 1980, we did not visit Amritsar. I have no idea why this was the case. It was probably that all contact had been broken and the immediate family members had died. Also, it is the responsibility of the other family members to come and visit you, rather than the other way round. For whatever reason, during our first visit to India with Mum, I do not recall visiting the family in Amritsar.

Chapter 3

My Early Years in India

I am the second eldest of seven children. Satvant Singh is the eldest, who is two and a half years older than I am and Gurnam Singh is seven years younger. Parminder Kaur and Baljinder Kaur were my younger sisters in India. Since coming to the UK, Satvinder Kaur and Jaswinder Kaur were born. Although we the children were in compact living conditions in the same house in India, we did not have a great deal to do with each other, and even if we did then my memory is letting me down.

As far as I am aware, Soos, near Hoshiarpur, Punjab, was the home of my paternal family, but I do not recall any memories of living there. I must have been very young living in that unreachable, isolated village. Having been born into the Sikh family, many religious ceremonies had to be performed. These could be either a full ceremony or a part ceremony. As to which one would have been performed at my birth, I have no idea and I suppose it did not matter. The parents of the child decide whether it would be a part ceremony or a full ceremony but most of the time it depends upon the financial position of the family and if the family wants to show off their wealthy position to the community, then it would be a full ceremony. Therefore, in our family, I suppose for most of us, if not all of us, we would have had a part ceremony. As a child, I attended one of these children naming ceremonies in Jandiala and this I can bring back to my memory. In this particular case, they set up the Gurdwara in the home of the parents. The parents would ask a Sant (a Sikh Priest), who would advise them on the ceremony and on the money to be paid for performing the ceremony. If it was to be a full ceremony, the whole of the Guru Granth Sahib, the Sikh Holy Book, would be read and that would take about a week for the complete ceremony to be performed. The Guru Granth Sahib would be read from cover to cover by several Sants who would take it in turns to read. Then, once it has been decided on the type of ceremony and where it is to be held, including the times, it would then take place. The family would decide on which day and time they would like to conclude the ceremony and then the timing would be calculated backward. I am assuming that one of these ceremonies would have taken place for all of us. During the concluding part of the ceremony, the Sant would close the Holy Book and then reopens it again, and then without looking, he would place his finger randomly at a word in the Holy Book. The first letter of that word would be used to name the child. In my case, it would have been J's equivalent in Punjabi, as my given name was Jagir. This was then shortened to Gogi which became my nickname. The ceremony would then be followed by food and celebration.

Within the Indian culture, boys hold a higher status than girls. Boys are strong and they can do hard manual work on the farms. Families will do all they can to educate the boys because they will become wage earners. They will support the family financially. On the other hand, girls are seen as inferior because they will require a wedding dowry which can be a great burden for the families. They will leave the family home following their wedding.

In Jandiala, although I got on reasonably well with the others in the family, there was always tension between one of my siblings and me. There was sibling rivalry. We both wanted to be the top dogs in the family and so frequently, we would argue over minor things. Although these things seem insignificant now, they mattered to both of us at the time. I, being older than her and being a boy, would rarely see eye to eye with her. On at least one occasion Mum said to me that the best thing to do was to avoid her. She then went on to explain that if she came into the same room as I was in, which was not difficult, then the best thing to do was to walk out. I did this on several occasions, then questioned as to why it should always be me who has to leave. These arguments continued as they usually did. With hindsight, these arguments were over trifling things that didn't matter but obviously, they did at the time. Sometimes you wish you could turn the clock back but life goes on. I do recall looking after Gurnam on several occasions and giving him some of my sweets and making sure he was alright. This is not something he would remember being so young. In terms of child care, it was a family responsibility, so whoever happens to be there took on the care of the younger ones. It was not a great deal.

Chapter 4

My Maternal Family

As far as I am aware, I was born in Soos, as this is the village recorded on my passport. Well, not Soos but Susan. The official wording is Soos. It's impossible to get the right pronunciation in a different language and that is why it's written as Susan. I must have been very young when my parents went to live in Jandiala village, near Jalandhar, in Punjab permanently. Most of my childhood memories are of being in Jandiala and of my maternal extended family. My parents, Swaran Kaur Raju and Kishan Singh Kalu married when my mother was only 14 years of age. From my calculations, the wedding would have taken place in 1936. She would have had no choice if she wanted to marry my father or not. Once, it had been agreed by the respective families, including the middle man, the wedding went ahead. The dowry was also agreed upon by the middle person. This was the custom in those days and it still is, except the rules are a bit more relaxed nowadays, especially in the cities. The agreement has to go ahead but if the agreement is broken, then the whole issue becomes a major problem leading to family dishonour. This was not the case between my maternal and paternal families.

My mother also had a younger brother, whose name was Sarwan Singh Raju and he was born in 1925. In those days birth dates were not seen as being important as they are today and were not always accurately recorded. So, it did not matter a great deal what date was recorded on the birth certificate, that is if you had bothered to get it recorded and to get a birth certificate. The birth registry offices are mainly located in the main cities. Sarwan Singh was fairly well educated; presume up to the tenth grade at school as he was able to write Punjabi, Urdu, and up to a point in English. My main memory of him was working in the shop and fetching the goods for the shop on his bicycle or Tonga. He was a gentle and very caring person. He thought the world of my mother. There was nothing that he would not do for her. He married Naseeb Kaur and together they had four children. The eldest was Daljit Singh, born on 2nd April 1955. Sadly, he died on 19th March 2017. The second eldest Amrik Singh came into the world on 1st April 1958. This was then followed by another boy, Jasvir Singh, he too was born on 1st April 1962 followed by Rani, a girl, who was born on 1st April 1963. You will see from the DOB's that all the children's births are recorded at the beginning of April. I can say with confidence that these are not the actual dates on which they were born. These dates were chosen to align with the school academic year. Most of the time, the parents don't even know the dates of their children's birthdays. However, most of them will know the year.

My maternal grandfather's name was Amar Singh Raju. As a family, they are of Sikh background. He was the third eldest of four brothers. The eldest's name was Avtar Singh Raju and this was followed by the next eldest. We, as a family, do not know much about him. We do not even know his name and we believe he died as a baby, during birth, or a miscarriage. The next to be born was my grandfather and then the youngest whose name was Jeevan Singh Raju. I can only remember my grandfather and Avtar Singh. Avtar Singh was a well-educated man who had contacts in high places. He was wheeling and dealing with people of high caliber and positions, such as Jewar Lal Nehru, Darbar Singh who following the election after the independence of India in 1947 became a Member of the Punjab State Parliament. He belonged to the Congress Party. Avtar Singh was an excellent walker. He would rarely jump on a public transport bus. He preferred to walk or go in a car. He was also a very stubborn and proud man and he would fall out with his family frequently over trivial matters. Following arguments, he would travel to the Golden Temple in Amritsar and after a week or two, he would return home when things have cooled down a bit. He enjoyed his independence. I only knew him as a widower. From time to time, he would make pakoras (Indian Savoury snack) which he would then sell. Avtar Singh had two sons; Sadhu Singh Raju being the eldest and Shev Singh Raju the youngest.

My granddad's youngest brother was called Jeevan Singh Raju. As the story goes, which I find quite amusing, he had an arranged marriage to one of the two sisters. This marriage was officially recorded with the registrar followed by a ceremony at the local Gurdwara for the customary religious ceremony and the blessings for the young couple. Within a few weeks of the wedding, his wife unexpectedly died. However, both his family and his late wife's family agreed for her sister Khami to be married to him. Following this decision, there was only a brief wedding ceremony at the Gurdwara. For financial reasons, the family decided not to have this marriage officially registered. So, legally they were cohabitating together. This was the first in our extended family. Khami was a very hot-tempered woman and she would stand no-nonsense. My memories of her are that she would spend almost all day sitting on her manja (bed) outside the house in the sun. I cannot recall her doing any housework. She would sit there all day swearing, shouting, and ordering the other women. She was extremely demanding and hot tempered. She was also a hypochondriac and would complain and moan every day about her health and others.

Khami's son, whose name was Darshan Singh, was also a weaver and he worked from home as most of the weavers did. He was a drug addict and suffered from ill health. He died early due to his addiction. For no apparent reason, we did not have much to do with this family but they were always pleased to see us.

My maternal granddad, Amar Singh Raju, was born in 1890 and he died at the age of 90. His wife, my grandmother Dhano Kaur, was born in 1897 and she also died at the age of 90 years. I have very fond memories of both of them as I will explain later on. Together they only had two children, one being my mother and the other my uncle Sarwan Singh Raju.

I have heard from a very reliable source how the wedding of my uncle Sarwan Singh and his wife Naseeb Kaur came about. This is how the story goes. My parents moved from Soos to Jandiala for economic reasons when I was very young. My father was in the weaving trade but was not doing well, so during the harvest season, he would travel around Punjab looking for farming work. On one of these occasions together with one or two other work colleagues, they were walking along a dusty foot path near Keengra, looking for work but found none and had very little money in their pockets. The evening was approaching and they had not eaten all day and had nowhere to rest for the night. They sounded miserable but somehow they met a stranger who was also walking toward his village. They got into conversation with this stranger for no apparent reason. The stranger asked them where their village was and how far they were walking. They explained their situation and how they travelled on foot looking for work but had found none. They had no village in mind to go to and nowhere to stay. This stranger pitied them and invited them to spend the night with his family. They were very happy with that offer knowing they had somewhere to stop where they would be fed. They accepted the invitation immediately. During their evening conversation whilst they were eating, this stranger mentioned to them that they were looking for a suitor for one of their daughters. Having given it some thought, they thought about my uncle Sarwan Singh. Later on, the two families were introduced to each other by my father as the middle man. Having agreed to everything the wedding was arranged and they were later married. It was as simple as that. Sarwan Singh passed away on 5th January 2011 and his wife Naseeb Kaur passed away on 5th January 1997 at the age of 64 years. They had a happy marriage.

Daljit Singh, Sarwan's and Naseeb's eldest son was born in 1955. He had a very relaxed personality and he was always cheerful and joking. He was a joy to be with. He was always very helpful, not just to the family but also to the wider community. He was known in the village as the Doctor because he was practicing medicine. He was not qualified in that field but managed to attain very basic medical knowledge. During one of my visits to Jandiala, Daljit was working under the supervision of a qualified doctor in a private hospital. So, Daljit took us to the hospital to introduce us to his colleague. They took us into the operating theatre which was a sight to behold. The hygiene was very poor and I was informed that they did everything from a broken collar bone to heart surgery. I certainly would not like to be treated there for any of my misfortunes. He did not work there for too long. Daljit would hold his surgery in the store room adjacent to his father's shop. This is where people would visit him throughout the day and he would give them mainly pain killers such as paracetamol, antibiotics, and the odd injection where needed. Money was not his primary objective and if the patient did not have the resources for the treatment, he would still go ahead and give treatment. Very often, he would get paid at a later date or not at all. He was greatly respected by the wider community and he knew the community well. He was always talking and spending time with people. On one occasion, I accompanied him on one of his visits to a patient. The family had no income. They were living in a mud house, they had one cow and very basic cooking utensils and the accommodation consisted of one room. The lady needed a pain-killing injection which he willingly gave with no charge. Such was his generosity.

During one of our visits to Jandiala, we needed the services of a Notary to draw up a legal document. He took us to Noor Mahal which was about 10 miles away from where we lived, where the notary services were based. As soon as we reached the Notary offices, he spoke to several people who knew him. He just walked up to one of the people he knew and after a brief greeting, he explained what we required and the papers were drawn by the clerks within half an hour whilst we chatted. Once written, the papers required the legal stamp but the solicitor was not available till after lunch. As we waited for his return, the queue outside the solicitor's office began to form, and then it became quite long. When the solicitor returned from his lunch, Daljit saw him and exchanged greetings with him. Having done that, Daljit explained the reason for us being there. The solicitor said to Daljit to give him ten minutes and then just walk into my office. After few minutes, we walked into the Solicitor's office and within five minutes we walked out with the necessary documentation. Such was the respect people gave him. On another occasion, Satvant and I needed reserved train tickets from Jalandhar to Delhi. So we made our way to the station in Jalandhar. The ticket office was so overcrowded and people were pushing each other to reach one of the three windows to purchase the tickets. After some time we gave up and said that we will come back later on. As we discussed this, a friend of Daljit spotted him. After few minutes of greeting, he asked the reason for our visit and we explained the situation to him. His friend told us to wait there and he would call us into a private office. After few minutes, he waved us behind the barrier and we walked into a private office where we were offered refreshments which we declined and we were issued with the required tickets for our journey. We were in and out of the office within ten minutes.

On another occasion during our visit to India in 1990, with my wife Brenda and her sister Melanie, we wanted to buy some musical instruments, so he took us to Jalandhar on the bus. On the return journey, we came to the bus station in Jalandhar, all of us got on the bus except Daljit. We were all looking for him but he was nowhere to be seen. The bus started to move, but no Daljit. As the bus continued to accelerate, Daljit jumped on the bus and a big cheer went out for him. The bus had broken down and he was helping to push start the bus. This was his personality. He is greatly missed by the family. Daljit sadly died in 2017 from a multi-organ failure. Following a telephone call from India, we were told that Daljit was very ill and was suffering from many things. It will not be long before he will pass away. As soon as we were informed of this, Satvant and I started to make plans to go and visit him in India which we did. We had a good time with him and his family.

It was so good to see him. He never made a full recovery and he died shortly afterward. Following his death, we visited the family again in November 2017.

Amrik, the second eldest, is the hardest working. He has a much more serious personality and can be short-tempered. He likes to be in control and likes to know what is going on all the time. He is a buyer and seller of material bedding and has managed to make a very good living.

Jasvir is the youngest boy and he is in the Police force in Delhi. He also has a very relaxed personality. Now, here is the story of how he joined the Police Department. Jasvir's uncle, a few years ago was working in a similar position to that of a Chief Constable of the Police Department. As Jasvir was having difficulty finding employment, his uncle suggested joining the Police Department and asked Jasvir to apply for a position which he did along with several other candidates. His uncle said that he will be offered a position. To join the Police department, you not only have to apply but also must pass a written exam. Unfortunately, Jasvir failed. So, his uncle took the application of a successful candidate and sent it to Jasvir. The successful candidate who did well at the examination was turned down. Therefore, all Jasvir had to do was to change his name to that of the successful candidate. So, Jasvir is no longer called Jasvir but Nirmal. With his uncle being the Chief of Police, Jasvir would turn up for work as and when he pleased.

Rani has a lovely personality. She is married to Gurdeep Singh and they have a boy and a girl. They are now both grown up and are a credit to their parents. They live near Hoshiarpur.

Rani is a housewife and Gurdeep was working as a Warehouse Manager on the outskirts of Phagwara in Punjab. He retired in February 2020. From this warehouse, sacks of wheat, rice, barley, and similar other food goods are distributed in the whole state of Punjab. He had several people working for him. He had the opportunity to travel abroad. He seems to have enjoyed his job. Their family house is halfway between Amritsar and Phagwara. During our family visit to India with Emma, my daughter, her husband Tim and their family, they welcomed us into their house. Their house was a good place to stop and take some refreshments which were most welcomed. Since we visited them in April 2018, their daughter has got married. Their son Supinder is now studying in Berlin, Germany. They are a lovely family with an easy-going personality. During our family visit to India, they took us to Havali village and a restaurant. It was a very enjoyable experience and very authentic.

Chapter 5

Life in Jandiala -
My Village

As it began to get light and the mist began to disperse, the day became less chilly on that memorable morning in 1953. It seemed the dawn of another normal day in my life. It was as if nothing had happened. After the hustle and bustle of that early morning, no one ever spoke of that day again and no one asked any questions. During the coming days, weeks, and months, life carried on as normal as if nothing had happened.

I began to realise that although living in India was quite fun, it had its ups and downs. There were more downs than ups. Jandiala, my village, was about 12 miles from Jalandhar the main city. It was quite a poverty-stricken village, with narrow, straight streets and open gullies running along both sides for sewerage and rain water. I can recall the main streets being paved and the gullies being built. Before this, the sewerage and the rain water would just run down the street. The hygiene was extremely poor and this seemed nothing unusual to us. This is how I remember the streets and treading in the sewage whenever I tripped. To fund the cost of the paved streets and the gullies, money was raised by the villagers themselves. Committee members went from house to house and shop to shop asking for contributions. When sufficient funds had been raised, the work started. These small narrow streets criss crossed each other and the main street was where most of the action took place that's if you could call it action because not a great deal happened.

The house which we occupied was off one of the main streets which were no longer than about 25 yards and our house was the end house. It had a small foyer measuring about 8 feet by 8 feet with a small brick floor but no roof. This was the main entrance space which was also used for cooking in the open. This was where Mum kept the chulla which is a small clay cooker with three or four legs at the bottom. Underneath the chulla, she would put some firewood or cow pats and then use the top of the chulla with a tawa on it to cook chapattis, parathas, and vegetable curries. Oh the food, the smell of it. I can still sense the smell. When it rained, she would pick up this very hot earthen clay object, the chulla, and take it inside and continue as if nothing had happened. Right above the chulla there was a small ladder. It was worn with some of the rungs missing and above all, it did not reach the roof, so the last couple of rungs I had to push myself up and climb over the ledge of the roof. In hindsight, it was quite a dangerous thing to do, bearing in mind, that I was only about 5 years of age at the time but I could do it. As I reached almost the top of the ladder on the right-hand side was the main door, which had a padlock and chain fitted. The only way of reaching this lock and undoing it was to climb up to almost the full height of this ladder, grip the edge of the roof ledge, and then reach across to the right as far as I could by leaning towards it without breaking my neck at full stretch and putting my right foot across the chain and turning the key with the right hand, because, the left hand I would use to steady myself up and unlock the padlock. My second aim as always was to get on the flat roof without breaking my neck. I became quite an expert in managing that. As well as the roofless foyer, our house also had two other rooms which were small, dark, and dingy. The first room was a work room where Dad did his weaving, as he was a weaver by trade. The second room was at the end of the first room. Both of these rooms were used as living rooms as well as for sleeping. These rooms were infested with mice, rats, and lizards. These rooms were all used by all of us as a family. There was no other space except a small 6 feet square space used for storage and cooking when it was raining. Later on, our accommodation took a turn for the worse. As our granddad and the rest of his family were struggling to run their family business, they brought a horse so that they could use the horse as a means of transport for fetching goods, for weddings, taxis, etc. Guess where the horse was kept at night. Yes, you guessed it right; it was in the foyer, which was the entrance to our little house. I can remember the food being cooked with the horse next to it. Now you can imagine our circumstances of sharing the basics of daily life with homegrown manure. You can't beat it. Talk about hygiene!

Having said all this, in comparison to the accommodation in Susa, it was luxury. We appreciated our house in Jandiala and the support we had from our uncle and our maternal grandparents as well as our other aunts and uncles. As a family, they were very kind to us.

This house was situated within a couple of minutes' walk away from the local well. There were only three wells in the village that I can recall. This water was mainly used for drinking and washing our dishes and pans as well as some laundry. As we did not have any running water and neither did anyone else in the village, this was the only way of getting some. This was very handy for us as a family due to the short distance to the well. The area around the well was very busy and a good gossiping point. This work was mainly done by women. Mum would go to the well carrying her buckets and the rope. She would tie the rope to the bucket handle and then sling it over the pulley which was supported by metal rails firmed in concrete around the well's outer circle for support. The bucket would drop to the bottom of the well making noises as it hit the sides of the well. It would fill up with water which appeared to be clean. It was cold and refreshing but I am aware now that it must have been contaminated with germs and all sorts of diseases. She would then pull the bucket up from the bottom of the well and transfer this water into another bucket so that the same bucket can be reused to fill up another container. Thus was life. Around the village well, some people would wash their laundry and as they did this, they would gossip. All the ladies knew each other and their businesses and this would also help to pass the time away and some of the miseries that they endured every day. This village well is no longer there and the site has been built upon. This place was a landmark for our community.

After Dad had left for England, life carried on as normal as if nothing had happened. I suppose in some ways nothing had changed as I do not remember Dad in India at all, except for one incident for which I am still carrying the scars. This incident I will never forget as it is ingrained in my memory. I must have been about four years old at the time. All I know is that I was quite stubborn in my early years as I recall swearing and shouting and being disobedient most of the time. Yes, I do recall this, but I don't recall being like this when Dad was at home. That broken ladder with the missing rungs played a vital role in my life. On just one occasion when I must have upset Dad so much that he held me upside down by my legs and suspended me as he stood and leaned over the ledge of the flat roof. I remember being there hanging upside down and crying, being suspended by my legs but not frightened. I was still carrying on with my usual stubborn behaviour and not giving in. There was no stopping in me. It made no difference. However, I do remember during this incident, my face being hit hard against the corner of the roof ledge. The cut must have been quite severe with the blood gushing out. I could feel no pain. How it missed my left eye I just do not know. I could have been blinded. I was still there hanging but stubborn as ever. As a result of that incident, I now have a scar on the corner of my left eye. Apart from that I have very few memories of Dad either talking to me or doing anything else with me. I don't even recall taking a walk with him or being in his arms. No memories but total voidness of his presence. I suppose this must be the reason why we never developed a relationship in India or England.

Dad worked from home. By caste, he was a Jalaha and therefore a weaver. He employed that skill well. He was not the only weaver in the village but there were several of them. They would weave thick sheets or bedspreads with different designs and patterns. Setting up the weaving loom was quite tricky and time-consuming. First, they would unravel and roll the cotton over thick sticks. Then they would start preparing the loom. To do this, they would insert several cane sticks into the ground in pairs over several yards. Once this has been done then they would loop the cotton numerous times from the thick stick over the cane sticks. The number of loops depended upon the width of the cloth that was to be made. Once this had been done, then came the complex part because the loom now had to be removed from the sticks, avoiding any tangles, and transferred to the manual weaving mechanism which was set up in the living room and was very intricate. Once the loom has been set up, the cloth could be weaved. The weaving mechanism consisted of a big pit in the ground which was in our living room. At a guess, the pit must have been about 4 feet square and about 4 feet in depth. The end of the loom was at the bottom of the pit with numerous looms coming up. Also at the bottom of the pit, were several foot pedals which Dad would press to get different patterns and to criss-cross the threads in place. Once he had pressed several pedals, he would throw the shuttle from one end to the other width way and he would then use a combing mechanism to lock and gather the threads in place. It was quite a tedious task but this was his trade and his living. Just outside the entrance to our house was a big flat stone about four feet by three feet and about twelve inches high firmed in the ground. It was heavy and set in place and could not be moved. It seemed a permanent fixture. This stone was used to soften the cloth once it has been weaved but it was there for other purposes too. The quality of the cloth was measured by its weight. The heavier the cloth the more expensive it was. So to gain extra weight they would soak the cloth once it has been woven in rich salty water and then leave it to dry. Once it was dry it would be as hard as a cucumber and difficult to fold, and this could only be done with some help. Once dry, they would then soften the cloth by hitting it with a heavy thick round stick over this stone. By doing this they would gain extra weight and thus gain extra cash. Although I knew about the process of weaving, I can only recall Dad working as a weaver about three times which was late into the evenings whilst he was in Jandiala.

As a youngster, I can remember going to school for the first time. I was quite nervous but at the same time looking forward to it. I remember walking to school with Mama who took me and registered me. I was just left there in the morning and had to stay there all day. There was nothing of this being slowly introduced to the school. I made few friends but the whole experience at the beginning was very strange. We had lessons in the morning. These were mainly maths and writings in Punjabi. Each of us had to have our fatti, which was used for writing. Having your fatti was a proud experience. Fatti was a flat piece of plywood about a quarter of an inch thick with a small handle cut out at the top. It measured approximately 12" x 10". We had to prepare the fatti each afternoon after school. We would wash it and then put some whitewash on it on both sides and then leave it to dry. We would take this to school each day and this would be used for writing lessons in Punjabi. If you made mistakes as you were writing, you could not rub it off and start again. It was there, mistake or no mistake until you took it home and prepared it again for the following day. Sometimes, we would use this for playing and chasing each other around with it. For maths, we had to use slates which we would wipe again and again several times a day. All this saved paper which we could ill afford. We were not the only family who did this but it was the custom at school. There must have been fifteen to twenty pupils in each class. We had to sit on the ground in rows outside under the trees. Several classes would sit outside every day and be taught. This was normal practice. The teacher would shout some numbers which came into his head and would ask the class to write them down which we faithfully did. Then he would shout some more numbers and some more and more and he then would ask us to add them all up. Sometimes he would ask us to subtract, divide or multiply. If you were to get these wrong which you would on numerous occasions, you were in for the cane. Every day several pupils would be caned. I remember being caned numerous times. This was the norm; you get used to it and so did the other pupils. There was no shame in being caned because you just took it as part of your learning experience. We were mainly taught maths and to write Punjabi at the junior school. In the afternoon quite often we would play games. At the end of each year, we had to take our exams to see how well we did. You had to pass the end of the year exams and if you did not, then you had to stay in the same class the following year. You could not progress any further until you have passed all of them.

The school had about five classrooms which were built of bricks. The rooms were shabby and very bare and on the outside people would write slogans, such as "Never leave anything until tomorrow if you can do it today". There were several of these slogans. The classrooms were of a single storey, like huts, quite dark, no electric lights except for a couple of windows to let the light through. Inside there were hardly any desks or other equipment except a blackboard and chalk.

The school also had a well on its grounds which was extremely useful. There were no health and safety barriers and often we, the children would look inside or climb the water wheel just for fun. If you slipped or fell in, it could have been fatal. The water wheel supported the small buckets which would fill up with water. The wheel was driven by some gears and a big handle which had to be pushed round and round. We, as boys, were exploited for our labour and we were told to push the wheel and water the veggie plots which were for staff use only. We would drink from that well during break time and lunchtime.

The infant school must have been about half a mile distance from home and we always walked except on the odd occasion when I would see my granddad on his Tonga. He would not stop, but he would ask us to chase it and then jump at the back of his Tonga. This was great fun. I enjoyed school and I made several close friends with whom I would play when there was time and my daily tasks had been completed.

On the way to school, I had to pass a small open slaughter area, which belonged to the local butcher, or at least he used it. This was an open yard nearby and within close vicinity of the shops and only a few yards from where my aunt and uncle lived. It was quite a busy area, set off the main road but it was not crowded by any means. Numerous people would pass by it as they went to school, for the latrine, to the farms, for family visits, and so on. This open yard had a good, strong permanent wooden pole firmed into the ground and every so often the butcher would use it to slaughter a goat. It was quite a sight for passersby and the hangers-on. The slaughtering would take place in the morning around the time we were on our way to school. When this was taking place, we boys would always hang around and watch. We would see the butcher pulling the goat by its horns toward the wooden pole. The goat would pull against the butcher because the goat knew where she was being taken to. The goat would sense it and would put up strong resistance but to no avail. The butcher would tie the head and the horns of the goat with a strong rope to the pole and the hind legs to the second pole. We would just stand there with our eyes open wide with a feeling of fear, anticipation, and almost being sick. The butcher would then take out his sword, stand with legs apart and fully stretched, he would lift his sword as far as he could, and then with all his mighty strength, he would bring the sword on the head of the goat to behead the animal. The head was then severed from the main body. There would be two pieces of flesh lying on the ground with the blood gushing like a fountain of water springing out from nowhere. The ground would be flooded in blood and you would be able to see its effects for several days. Once the head had been severed, the whole body would continue to move for several seconds. The main body of the animal would try to stand up, but with little effect, until it gave up. Part of the head would also move until its life had almost evaporated from both parts of the body. Even after that, there would be the odd spasm of movement until it was no more. As boys, our curiosity was fulfilled but at the same time, a tragic sight to behold and see an animal suffering in such a way, but as boys, we were curious to watch this, even if we were going to be late for school which we often were.

Another memory I have of my time at the primary school is one which I had mentioned previously that we were not that well off in India. No one was and we were all struggling to survive. It was a very hot summer day and I went to school without shoes or sandals which I could not find. Walking to school barefoot in the morning was not a problem as the sun had not drenched its heat on the ground. However, walking back from school was a different story having no shoes or sandals on my feet. It was not a big problem when I started home from school as there were few patches of grass here and there and I would step on them so I could cool my feet. However, for part of that journey home, there was no grass at all and the soil was covered with dust and stones and some concrete. The ground was extremely dry and hot and every step I took would burn my feet. I had to find small patches of grass to walk on and from time to time I would take several steps so that I could reach the next small tuft of grass quickly. My feet were burned by the time I got home and I could hardly walk. This was the last time that I ventured to school with no coverings for my feet. A lesson truly learned and never to be repeated or forgotten.

At school, every year I passed all my annual exams and then enrolled at the local high school to do my fifth year and onward studies. There were two high schools in Jandiala village, one being the Republic High School and the other one the Communist High School I think. They both competed against each other. I was enrolled at the Republic School where most of our family went. The Republic High School was a bit further away than the infant school. Getting there was not a problem because as youngsters we had plenty of energy to disperse. Here we had some classes outside in the sun and some inside. The rooms were similar to the ones I occupied in the junior school, but in a better condition and with more windows which gave more light and ventilation. It also had a small play area outside containing a slide and a swing and a roundabout which we could use. This was very unusual as we had not seen equipment like that before. The classrooms were plain with no equipment or resources in the room except a blackboard. They were very basic. Again, the discipline was similar to the one applied at the junior school. I got the cane several times but often it was a block punishment for the whole class. You don't know what you have done but you were punished. Instead of a cane, the other punishment they used was quite humiliating and painful. We had to bend forward and then crouch on our legs and put our hands through the back of our legs and then hold our ears. It was ok for a minute or two but any longer than that was quite painful. This was quite a regular occurrence for everyone at school. At the end of the academic year, I passed my fifth year and progressed to the sixth year. The fifth-year standard of education was nationally recognised as it was of a reasonable standard.

I started my sixth year at school quite well and knew that I was doing fine. During that year I became quite friendly with another boy and we would often have lunch together. We would find a small tuft of dry grass under a small sapling with no leaves. Although the grass was all dry and hard at least it kept our pyjama bottoms clean. The sun was always beating on our brow. To find a little shade of a parched tree was like gold. He never brought any lunch with him. It transpired that his family was extremely poor and they could not afford a great deal of food. They must have struggled to fund his education. He must have had brothers and sisters but he rarely mentioned them. So I remember sharing my lunch with him frequently. He was a great lad and he never complained about anything but he would always wait for me especially at lunchtime. I did not complete my sixth year but left school halfway to come to new pastures in the UK. School in a way mattered very little because I did not have to take any exams. I continued to work hard at school.

With Dad not being around and the money being scarce or nonexistent, we were brought up by our maternal grandparents and aunt and uncle especially uncle Sarwan, my mother's youngest brother. They were always there for us, supporting us, providing for us and caring for us, and meeting all our needs. Our maternal family, including our aunts and uncles, were our family. As a family, we owe a great debt to them all. They were like a father and mother to us all and nothing seemed to be a great deal of trouble to them regardless of the time of day or night. They have our admiration and respect. As I mentioned earlier, the house that we occupied in Jandiala belonged to our maternal family. Uncle Sarwan and our maternal granddad made their living as shopkeepers. They occupied a small grocery store, which sold almost everything you could think of. They mainly sold tea, sugar, cooking oil, flour, and various types of lentils, atta, spices, etc. They would buy in bulk and then transport all these goods from Jalandhar to Jandiala. In the early days, my uncle would cycle to Jalandhar, load up his bicycle, and then do the 14-mile return journey home. This was an all-day trip after which he would be tired and worn amidst the unbearable heat in the summer, wet and cold during the monsoon. It was hard work for him and when he was doing this, the shop would be managed by our granddad who suffered from severe asthma attacks. He was always coughing and spluttering all the time and would have great difficulty breathing. It was difficult for him to rush anywhere but he was always on the go, never stopping. It was obvious that he was getting old, tired, and worn out. It became very difficult for uncle to transport the goods from Jalandhar and to run the shop at the same time. They were able to make a living from the shop, but the future was not very bright, so they decided to buy a horse and to have a Tonga. This was a great venture for them. They would use the horse and Tonga for transporting shop goods from Jalandhar to avoid using the bicycle which was very hard work. The Tonga could be used by granddad for fetching the goods which he was more than capable of doing. In addition to this, Tonga could be used for other occasions such as a taxi, for weddings, transporting goods for other small businesses, and so on. This is how we ended up having a horse in our back garden or more to the point in our foyer. The horse had to be fed and watered. It had to be looked after. Uncle and granddad then acquired a small field about twenty minutes walk from our shop. This responsibility was passed on to my brother Satvant and me. Every afternoon after school we would take a sheet or a blanket and a scythe and walk to the field, cut the green for the horse, wrap it all up in a sheet and knot it at the four corners and put it on our head and carry it back to the house for it to be prepared. There were times when it was a struggle to carry it back. The green would then be fed into the feed cutting machine which was driven manually and rotated by the handle. It was then ready to be given to the horse. This was a daily routine task that had to be performed, regardless of the weather or time.

When we were not at school during the summer vacation, and not looking after the horse, we would serve in the shop. This was our daily task and we were expected to do it without any question. We enjoyed doing it. I would weigh the goods as requested and then sell them. Over time, I must have spent numerous months serving the customers in the shop. On one occasion, we were sitting just a few yards away from the shop, when a customer entered the shop. As we came back to serve him, he had hidden several tea sachets under his clothing. This was discovered. To ensure he was charged, my uncle and some other people accused him of stealing other things too. I don't know the outcome of what happened later, but immediately he was beaten and kicked by my uncle and other friends who were also shopkeepers. People were extremely poor and they took the opportunity when they could. Having said this, crime was not a major problem. There was nothing of what we get today with youths hanging around and shouting abuse at each other. We were not frightened to go out at night, knowing that we would be reasonably safe. The ferocious and hungry dogs were more of a problem than anything else. As youngsters, we were safe and we did not have anyone looking after us. We knew the people in the community. We could go out in the fields to play as we wished, as long as our tasks were completed. There was not a great deal of time to play but it was sufficient for our social needs.

As far as the shop was concerned, we acted responsibly and that was fine. Even when uncle was around, we would still look after the shop. Quite often uncle would play cards with the other shopkeepers, neighbours, and friends as that was a good way of occupying their time and when customers came, he would send us to serve. Playing cards was their daily entertainment without gambling; otherwise, their life would be so dull. This was the highlight of their day. The shop had to be cleaned every morning and this would be done either by my brother or me. This task had to be completed before going to school.

Although the shop and the care of the horse occupied a substantial amount of our time, there were other fun and family times too. I remember going to Jalandhar and Nakodhar on different occasions to purchase goods for the shop with my granddad. They were similar distances apart but in the opposite direction. We would set off very early in the morning as the day would be breaking; it would be cold and chilly and we would wrap a kambal, a blanket around ourselves together, which would cover our whole body including our heads and we would try to keep warm. As the dawn would break, and the sun would emerge over the horizon, it would begin to get warm and then gradually very hot. The heat was not a major problem for us on these occasions, because we would catch the breeze as the horse galloped pulling Tonga behind him. This was great as we were independent, whilst others we saw running to catch the cramped buses and people rushing everywhere, pulling and brushing past each other to jump on the bus or the rickshaw. On the odd occasion, whilst travelling to these destinations we would pick up other paying passengers. In Jalandhar, our main destination was the mandi, which was the wholesale market. We would ride with our Tonga straight into the centre of mandi and would then try to find somewhere to park which was difficult at times. Granddad would then leave me in charge of Tonga and the horse and he would go and see one of the wholesale brokers, who would order the goods for him from several different stores. It had to be done through him and his commission paid. This task would take him about an hour but to me, it seemed several hours.

I am sure it must have been about a couple of hours. Once the goods had been ordered, we would take the Tonga to the various outlet huts in the mandi and they would load the ordered goods on the Tonga. Then would come the treat, we may call in at a soda shop or get some kulfi (Indian ice cream) or something else similar. I always looked forward to that. Having done, what we had to do, then we would ride back to our village. This was a great day's outing. On one of these occasions, the weather was bad but the journey still had to be made to Jalandhar and I was accompanying granddad on this occasion. We got there without much difficulty and loaded our Tonga with the goods as we had done previously which was now a routine. On the return journey, it had been raining very badly and the road was very slippery for most of the way and the horse was struggling to pull the Tonga in the mud. We even got off the Tonga and walked for quite a long distance. The journey was very difficult. It began to get dark and in India, it gets dark very quickly and there are no street lights except hazards for which you have to look out for. Before we could reach the village and about a couple of miles to go, the horse slipped and fell due to the mud. In the fall, the horse broke one of its legs and we were stranded. As we were so late in returning to the village, our uncle came out looking for us and so the help was at hand. Both uncle and granddad took advice from other people and it was decided to put the horse out of its misery and the horse was shot. This was quite a sad day and a very expensive one too. The horse was replaced a few months later so that they could continue trading.

As a youngster, I use to look forward to going out with my maternal granddad and I knew he would look after me. Life in the village was quite boring as nothing much happened. If I could go with him, then this would break the monotony of being in the village all the time. One day he was going to see some relatives who lived not far away for few days. He casually asked if I would like to go with him. My response was immediately very positive. Initially, he was going in the morning, and then the delays followed as it usually does. We call it India time. I am not sure if there were delays in his arrangements or if he was working to an Indian time. The morning went by and then came the afternoon and I was hanging around to make sure that he didn't go without me. As there did not seem to be a great deal of progress, I went for a walk with some of my friends and together we were just messing about and whilst there, we picked up some poppies for no apparent reason. At my friend's house we got some water and boiled the poppies, added some sugar and then drank the juice. After a short time, I became so tired and sleepy and dizzy. I eventually made my way back home with some difficulty and fell asleep on the manja. That was all I wanted to do, as I had no energy to do anything else. I was knocked out completely. Having fallen asleep, I remember my head spinning and then eventually waking up. I again wanted to go to sleep and do nothing else. Then I suddenly remembered, that I am supposed to be going with my granddad to see some relatives. I had no idea if he had gone or not but deeply hoping that he had not. As I was coming round, I had no idea at all what time of the day it was, was it the morning, evening, or even mid-day, or for how many days I had slept. I was completely disorientated. There was no clock by which I could check the time and I was too scared to ask anyone else as I didn't want them to know my state and how awful I was feeling. I was on the verge of being sick and if they knew how I was feeling, then I would not be able to go with granddad for few days, that is if he had not already left. It was quite a dilemma. I have no idea if I went with him or not, but I do know that he had not left by the time I was beginning to get back my senses and my common sense.

Being with granddad was great. I also remember going with him on his political campaign. I must have been around seven or eight years old at that time. It was election time and the two major political parties contending were the communist party and the congress party. Our family and the extended family, meaning our aunts and uncles including our great aunts and uncles were supporters of the congress party. You have to remember that this time was soon after the partition between India and East and West Pakistan and also soon after India had attained its independence from the British Government. So the political situation was quite fragile. I remember going with granddad and other Congress party campaigners, standing in the back of the trailer, which was being pulled with a tractor. Talk about health and safety; we were being thrown from side to side as we travelled on the rough roads around Jandiala. I had difficulty trying to see over the sides of the trailer due to being so young. The tractor went to different parts of Jandiala and also to another village to sound their political message.

Our great uncle Avtar, my paternal granddad's brother was a friend and supporter of Dalwara Singh, who became the local member of the Parliament. This politician later became the Prime Minister of Punjab or its equivalent. In 1980 on our return visit to India, we went to Chandigarh, the capital of Punjab, and whilst there great uncle Avtar decided to visit the Punjab Parliament building and visit Dalwara Singh. He had a brief word with the receptionist as you enter the building, who told him that Dalwara Singh was not in Chandigarh today. This was quite a disappointment for all of us.

In Jandiala, foul and strayed dogs were always strolling up and down the street and constantly barking. Some of these dogs were very dangerous, not so much because of their breed but because they were always hungry and then became aggressive in their character. They were difficult to contain. They were roaming the streets looking for scraps of food from wherever they could. They would often come to our house and bark at the door as the food was being prepared or being consumed. I remember, on one of these occasions my younger brother Gurnam being bitten on the arm by one of these dogs. This particular dog had rabies. This was a disaster as there were no medical facilities in the village or any antibiotics available in the village or anyone knowing how to deal with this emergency. In the village, about 50 yards away from our grocery shop lived a very, very poor family and the man's main job was to clean the streets, the gullies, etc. His cast was the lowest of low and thus was his job. I think they had three children, two boys, and a girl. He was also a snake charmer and if anyone was bitten by the snake, then he would try to suck out the poison with his mouth. At times he was successful and others not. He would suck out the poison, spit it out, and then he would take a mouthful of liquid ghee, refined unsalted butter, and would swallow that. When he had done that, he would repeat the same process again and again. Although my brother was not bitten by a snake, but by a rabid dog, there was no alternative but to try the same method on him. First, we had to find the snake charmer, which our uncle did with the help of others. The word spread quickly that someone had been bitten by a rabid dog and that our family was looking for this man. The ghee was no problem, although it was expensive, my uncle's shop had plenty in store and this ghee was then immediately delivered to his house. He began the painful and frightening process of depoisoning the arm where Gurnam had been bitten. Gurnam was screaming and had to be held down. It was extremely frightening to see all these people around him while he was shouting and screaming. This process was completed within minutes. The next step was to seek urgent medical attention at the nearest hospital. Although there was a hospital in the village, this kind of emergency was beyond their capabilities. So, the following day, Gurnam was taken to the hospital in Jalandhar where he received a course of injections. I think he had to have approximately twelve injections, once a day. Our uncle Sarwan and Mum would walk down to the railway station, catch the train and then a rickshaw and would arrive at the hospital about mid-day and then wait in the long queue in the open yard. Here you could hear children screaming and shouting, as they were injected against various diseases. The same needle, after it has been sterilised was used again and again. To sterilize the needles, they were boiled in water for several minutes and then reused. Quite often we would have to wait for the needles to be ready. Some of them were becoming blunt, so it was quite painful when you were being injected. Once he had been injected, then it was time to return home. It was a whole day job and very expensive due to transport and the course of injections. The whole process was physically and emotionally draining but it had to be done. He fully recovered having undergone the prescribed treatment.

In our spare time, late afternoon and into the evenings, we would play across the fields just by the main road which led to Jalandhar. This main road was no more than a dirt track and the main mode of transport was the bicycle or a gadda, a cart being pulled by one or two cows. This cart would be loaded with hay or with other similar things. There was no risk of us being hit by a car or a lorry. It was safe for us to play. Quite often in the fields or on the main road, we would play hockey. The hockey stick was improvised by breaking a strong branch of a tree in the shape of hockey and then used. We could not afford a hockey stick. We were not the only ones in that situation but we still had great fun. We would run across the fields and play as we wished. We had full freedom to play outside without any risks.

One of our neighbours was Tarsam, who was a couple of years older than me. His family had a very small workshop next to our house, more like a spare room than a workshop. From time to time he would spend time making small musical instruments such as a very small keyboard, using odd wooden boxes and wires and whatever else he could lay his hands on. He was very successful at that. Occasionally, we would go with him into the fields, where he would play this instrument and we would all sing and laugh together. It was a lot of fun.

I recall seeing my first film ever. This was when a film was being shown in the village. We had to wait till the evening when it got dark. The film was screened in the middle of one of the streets and almost everyone in the village turned up to see it. I had no idea what a film was. It was completely amazing, overwhelming, to hear sound and to see people moving around on the screen. I thought that this may be a trick, so I went to look behind the screen to find out how it was done. I was completely puzzled and I could not work it out. These were the new inventions of those days.

From time to time, odd bits of my old memory crop up. I remember going with my maternal granddad to visit a family and staying there overnight. This family's neighbour had a gramophone player. I do not recall seeing one previously. It was very old. This neighbour put the vinyl on the machine and wound it up using a handle with the horn piece sticking up. The gramophone needle was a bit blunt, so he got a stone, and using the stone he sharpened the needle and then stuck it back into the arm of the turntable. I am sure some young people would not even accept that this was the technology we have been brought up with or may think we are making it up. This was normal for us as we lived in a village.

These are some of the many memories that I reflected upon as I began to put pen to paper. There are many more memories I could recall but they are too numerous to record. Generally, life carried on regardless of what we did or knew.

Chapter 6

Preparation for Departure to England

During my fifth year at the Republic High School in 1959, things began to take shape. That is when I realized that the world around us as a family may be changing. Would that be for the better or worse was the question. I did not know or care as living in a mundane environment in a village was not the future that I was looking forward to. So, joining my father and living with the whole family seemed a better option for all of us. Although I did not think much about what I would be doing after I had left school, considering what others were doing in our community who had a good education, the prospects did not seem to be that bright. So, all options except staying in Jandiala seemed a good choice, not only for me but for the whole family. Not that I had any other options or was asked for my opinion as to come to the UK and join Dad was completely out of my control.

As part of the preparation for our journey, the first thing that had to be sorted out was the passports. There was so much red tape in getting any legal documents, in fact, any document. All of us would be registered on to mum's passport. Getting a passport was even more difficult, as it would be the ultimate document acceptable in any country. Most of the time, people had to be bribed to attend to your paperwork. It was not what you know but who you know and with how much you can line their pocket with. It was complete bribery and corruption. The higher the position they held in the government, the more they expected. On some of these occasions, you would have to take an important member from your village to the meeting at the public offices in Jalandhar or Chandigarh, or New Delhi. The wait to see someone would be long and very often it would be the wrong queue and then you would have to wait at the back of a different queue. There was no rush to process any paperwork unless your bribe was significant. The forms would have to be completed in triplicate with carbon copies etc. The process was not as simple as filling in an application form and hoping it would get there and your passport would arrive about four weeks later. It was a long-winded process and quite often you would have to prove why you needed a passport and still be unsuccessful. Being unsuccessful was more frequent than being successful and then the whole process would start again. For the children's name to be placed on the passport, you needed a birth certificate or the equivalent thereof. All of my brother's and sister's births had been registered in Jalandhar except for mine. There were mega problems for my name to go on my mother's passport. All the birth records were checked and checked again and there was no trace of me being born. I existed but could not prove it. It transpired that my birth was not registered in Jalandhar as it should have been, because I was born during the civil war in India in 1947 around the time of the independence. Atrocities were being committed between the Muslims and the remaining factions and religious groups. The Muslims wanted control of India and they also wanted a Muslim Prime Minister. It was horrendous. There was utter carnage, not that I saw any of this but it is well recorded in the historical documents. Murders were being committed and neighbours were fighting neighbours, having lived peacefully with each other previously for years. The neighbours were hacking each other down with swords and setting fire to their houses. The harvest fields were being set on fire and the complete crops were destroyed including the equipment. Numerous houses were burned on both sides. The Muslims would come into the village and they would use their swords and rampage the house, kill children, rape the women, and finally set fire to the houses. Many people in the community would go into hiding. The trains were being derailed and the carriages set on fire. This was a terrifying time and thousands of people lost their lives, their homes, their children, and their livelihood. This was not just one-sided. The villagers would take revenge on the Muslim area and their villages likewise. There was no way these differing religious factions would be able to live in harmony with each other. All this was taking place whilst India was gaining its independence in 1947, from under the control of the British Government. There was no place to hide and this was the situation throughout the country during the time of my birth.

Now then, coming back to why my birth was not registered, I was told by other members of the family that it was too dangerous to travel to Hoshiarpur to register my birth. There were no guarantees that the registration office would be open and which religious member of staff would be dealing with the registration of my birth. Also during troubled times, I was informed that to keep me safe as a baby my father had to escape with me to the fields and hide. I had no idea what was happening to the other members of the family and how they were surviving. I was too young to even think about it.

So it transpired that the family could not apply for my passport until the registration issue of my birth had been resolved. As I was now living in Jandiala, numerous visits had to be made to Jalandhar with important people from the village to speak on the family's behalf and after explanations, the officials eventually agreed to register my birth at the age of eleven years. The family had no idea as to the day, the date, or the month I was born in. At the Registration Office, they took out the birth register to register my birth but there was no space on the page around the time I was born, so they turned several pages in the registration book and eventually came to a page where there was a small space at the bottom of the page and my name was then placed on that line with indelible ink. Therefore, my birthday is now registered for 10th September 1947 but in reality, I have no idea when I was born and neither do my parents. When I tell other people that I don't know when I was born they have difficulty in believing and think that I am telling them a tale.

The one and only family passport was eventually acquired and the arrangements progressed for us to come to this country. My brother Satvant is older than me and he was going to be in his sixteenth year in April 1960. This also became a major issue that had to be resolved for the family before we could embark on making further arrangements. There is a big difference in the way you count people's age between India and the UK. As Satvant was going to be in his sixteenth year, the family was under the impression, that he would not be able to travel on the family passport and would therefore require his own passport. As mentioned earlier, obtaining another passport would be extremely difficult, costly as well as causing delays to our departure. Taking this into account, arrangements were hastily made for us to travel to the UK as soon as possible due to Satvant's birthday. The price of the air ticket was expensive and the cost was a big issue to resolve. So the family looked at the alternatives. They considered travelling by ship and discovered that this was even more expensive than by air. Based on this decision, my father then booked the air tickets for the whole family to come to the UK by air. Subsequently, as a result of that decision, I had to leave my school in the middle of the academic year and was therefore unable to complete my sixth year of education.

What I have not mentioned so far, is that the arrangements were also being made by our neighbouring family, who were in the same predicament as our family. A small but wealthier family than ourselves lived next door to us. Their house was adjacent to ours on the right-hand side and we shared an adjoining wall. They had a huge courtyard and larger rooms than we occupied. In the courtyard, they had a nalka, a water pump. There was no need for them to go to the nearest water well to fetch water as we had to. This house was occupied by our Mama and Mamee, our uncle and aunt. We were not related to them but we always called them Mama and Mamee as was the Indian custom to call them with respect. This family had lived there ever since I can remember. Mama and Mamee Ji had two children, Shindo, a girl, and Tarsam a boy. Shindo was the eldest. In the courtyard, they also had a cow that would provide milk for the family. This cow suffered unintentionally at their hand from time to time. I recall that on one occasion, this particular cow became extremely ill and there were no vets in the village, so they could not seek any medical help. However, numerous people advised them to administer various herbal medications via a blunt instrument in the shape of a shuttle through the nose. The cow objected very strongly. Then they tried administering the same herbal medication by tying the cow's neck to a pole and she continued to object very strongly. Having failed that, they then also tied her hind legs to the pole and still without success. One of the suggestions was that the cow was sick internally and therefore must be unclean. To ensure the cow is clean then we must give her soapy water. Not sure if they tried this or not. I could see several men trying to give the cow some sort of medication and the enormous struggle the cow put up. Then they tried the same medication through the throat without success and then finally through the cow's back passage. Sadly, the cow died after few days. As I mentioned earlier, they were not so poverty-stricken because they could afford a radio to which we would all listen in the evenings as the volume knob would be turned up by several notches. The radio was also a sign of their prosperity. The radio programmes were much appreciated by the whole of our family. Their grandfather would rise very early in the morning and he would bathe himself under the water pump and whilst doing so he would repeat his prayers. This was his ritual, which he carried out each morning to start the day right.

Saying his morning prayers were part of his good deed by which he would earn his salvation before God or at least that was what he thought. This was also an outward sign that he was a religious and devout Sikh. Then the rest of the day it would not matter what he thought or did. This was a ritual he would perform and he would let other families know about it by saying his prayers aloud. There was tension between our neighbouring family and our uncle's family as I recall. On one occasion, there was a physical fight amongst the men from both sides of the family. This was concerning the adjoining wall which was being shared by both of the families. They had carried out some building alterations in which this wall was involved and it had been done without any consultation. Following this fight, my uncle Sarwan gave me a note to take it to one of the doctors at the local hospital for some medication. He gave me strict instructions, not to show the note to anyone and to go to the hospital directly and return quickly. Their son Tarsam and I were good pals and we would very often play together. Tarsam and Shindo's father, Resham Singh also came to the UK several years previously. I reckon they must have travelled together or about the same time as my Dad to provide a living for his family and make his fortune in this country. Both Dad and Resham occupied the same house in Wolverhampton for several years. Regardless of that, the family feud continued for some time in Jandiala. They were also in the process of making arrangements for their family to come to the UK. Their documents had arrived and they were now able to book the tickets to come to England. As they say, there is strength in numbers, both the families agreed to travel together. It was better and economical to join forces and make the arrangements together, as we were all nervous because none of us spoke the English language or had ever flown previously. This was going to be a new game. We needed each other for comfort and support as we had several stopovers on the way and none of us could understand what was going on. This must have been very difficult for our mothers as they were illiterate and had the overall responsibility for looking after us on the long journey. There were several stops on the way. I recall drinking pop for the first time at one of the airports on the way. It was cold and it gave you a tingling feeling on your tongue. However, we managed with some help, and here I am now writing about it sixty years later.

Chapter 7

The Journey to England

Now that we had acquired our Passport for the whole family and other relevant documents such as visas, flight tickets, etc, other travel arrangements had to be made. We were ready to leave our small and insignificant village and venture out for new pastures. I was quite looking forward to this because as a youngster I was told by our neighbours and friends that I should be really happy as I was going to England. They would be more than willing to take my place if they had the opportunity. They would jump at it. England was the country where there is no poverty and the streets are lined with gold. So I would never be short of anything. As a youngster, I found this quite difficult to comprehend, how could the streets be lined with gold when the streets in our village are covered with dust and manure? How could there be a vast difference between the two places? Obviously, as a youngster, I could not comprehend the meaning of this phrase.

Weeks and months before our departure to England, there were lots of comings and goings. There were several problems and difficulties regarding our departure which I can no longer recall.

However, I do remember numerous relatives and friends coming to say their last farewell knowing they will not be seeing us for a long time. Every time the visitors arrived, we the children would go through the usual Indian customary greetings of bowing down and touching their feet or bowing down to them on all fours. The night before our departure to England hardly anybody slept.

Excited and full of joy, I looked forward to coming to England. However, the day before we left the village and ventured into the unknown was very sad, as we knew that we would never see some of our friends, relatives, and more importantly our schoolmates again. As the neighbours arrived we would greet them. Depending upon who they were, they would have to wait outside by the door until our Mammi, (auntie) would come and pour oil on the doorpost after which they would enter. This was a sign of welcome for important relatives. As youngsters, we had very little control over our destiny. Mum was sad and would often shed tears as she talked with the family, relatives, and friends about our future as a family. They all would ask us to write to them and to keep in contact and Mum knew that this would be an impossible task, but promises had to be made but not kept. On the day of our departure, we did not have to work in the shop but the horse still had to be taken care of which was done by the other family members. People would just come and go and more than half of them, I had never seen before or knew or even cared who they were. They had not bothered to come and see us before and therefore, they were not going to miss us now. However, it was their solemn duty within the Indian culture to show sadness and respect at our departure and we had to do the same if they were in our position. They all came out of the woodwork and carried out their duty to visit us before our departure had to be done. They would give mum a few rupees which she had a duty to decline and these rupees then would be accepted very reluctantly. On occasions, only part of that money would be accepted even though they could barely afford it. The customs and the culture play a significant part within the families, even if they had to go without food or other things. These duties are more important than the act itself. Unless these customs are carried out the honour within the family is questioned. It disgraces the family unless these are fulfilled. Disagreements between the families had to be overlooked when you are all together. The whole family was busy preparing food. Numerous curries had to be made to feed all the arrivals and the departures and chai were constantly boiling on the chulla. I remember going to see an elderly gentleman, Prakash Lal, who lived about fifty yards away from our shop. He was a devout Hindu. He would spend hours just talking to our uncle and our other relatives. I remember going to have a natter with him as he was such a lovely guy. He used to make Indian sweets such as paras, jalebis, laddu, barfi, and so on. He had lived in the village all his life and most of the people knew him. I should say most of my life because as far as I was concerned he had always lived there and always made Indian sweets. He was of the Brahmin caste, which is a high caste. He would dress in his white Dhoti and a collarless white shirt. He had extremely short hair except for few strands which were about eight inches long coming from the centre of his head and leaning backward. He would have a red dot painted on his forehead. He was loved and respected by everyone.

The day of our departure had arrived and now there was no turning back. Life was now getting exciting, apprehension or not. I was looking forward to what was coming next. The worse it could be, was that we would be back here and continue with our dull life. Both the families were dressed in their smart clothes, wearing bright coloured kameez and pyjama. We all looked very smart and posh. We had never looked that smart before even when we had to go to a family wedding. For our departure day, we all had new tailor-fit clothes made for our journey. The clothes were made by one of our cousins whose name was Sant. He was a professional tailor and he suffered from very severe scoliosis. He had a manual Singer sewing machine. He would sit on the floor all day and tailor. I suppose this did not help his already severe health condition but how else could he make a living? All our clothes were made to order by him. He and his family lived almost on the opposite corner of our shop.

A few days before our flight, we left our village to travel to New Delhi by train. There were about 30 people, including family members, neighbours, colleagues, and school friends who accompanied us to the local train station, which was about a mile, a mile and a half away. We all walked toward the station and the suitcases were placed on the Tonga, together with some elderly family members. As we walked we talked and made promises to keep in contact with each other. Some of our schoolmates accompanied us and we had a good natter about times past but there were also long silences because of the uncertainties of the future. As we walked we made promises to keep in touch with each other. We arrived at the railway station and then waited for the steam train to come from Nakodhar to Jalandhar. As we waited for the train, we said our final farewell to some of the people as they were not able to accompany us any further, especially our school friends. Accompanying us to Jalandhar on the train would also cost them financially. This was the end of their farewell. This was the end. As the steam train chuffed and puffed, gradually the wheels of the train came to a sudden halt. It was already overcrowded with passengers pushing each other to get on or off. There was no waiting to let the passengers get off the train. If you did, you would probably miss the train altogether. Several people helped us with luggage and we were scattered in different carriages due to the overcrowding. People were pushing and shoving each other. The train only stopped momentarily. We had to push ourselves onto the train and we had to pass our luggage to some of the passengers through the window. The train only stopped for few minutes and it made no difference to the driver whether you were on or off or only halfway on the train. The train would just go and it was your responsibility to make sure you were on the train and you were safe. There was no hanging about, except literally for those who were hanging on to the doors and still trying to get in. Once we were all on the train, then our uncle and other relatives had to collect the various suitcases from different carriages to make sure the luggage was completely safe and all together. As the train was being boarded, I remember another family with a young baby trying to board the train and they were having great difficulty due to overcrowding. They passed the baby through the window to another passenger and then just about managed to step on the train as the train began to pull towards its destination. He eventually managed to board the train. Just imagine what could have happened if he would not have been able to board the train. These difficulties were common and were expected. There were no complaints but you were grateful to be able to board the train. As far as I can remember, the trains were always approximately on time. They turned up within ten minutes of the expected time, not that I had a watch to compare it. I remember sitting on the train on that momentous day. The seats were arranged as a bench with slats. There was no cushioning for the seats and many people standing with nothing to hold on to when the train accelerated or slowed down within each carriage. There was so much pushing and shoving going on. It was a field day for pickpockets. I know that it was a steam train because that was all we had in those days. On some of these journeys, as we stood and the train accelerated, we would open the windows and let in some fresh air including some of the fumes, grits from the coal as well as some soot. On some of the journeys, our clothes would be covered with black soot. These days bring back memories of childhood and they will never be forgotten. As I write this, I can smell and taste the dregs of charcoal and soot in my mouth and relive the past.

Our train eventually arrived in Jalandhar and from there we had to catch another train which I suppose was to New Delhi. I do remember having some seats and nattering with the family and eating a paratha which was our packed lunch. From here my memory goes a bit blur, however, I do recall our great uncle Avtar Singh accompanying us on the train to Delhi. Several relatives were travelling to Delhi with us, so we knew we would be alright. As children, it was not our responsibility to get us to the airport and on the flight on time. Avtar was the main brain behind it. On the way, the train was calling at Ludhiana station. Great uncle Avtar had to visit a friend or a family member in Ludhiana after which he said he would join us in New Delhi. He didn't want to get a ticket for Ludhiana and then buy another ticket from Ludhiana to New Delhi. This would be very expensive and so he had to improvise a way of getting off the train and avoiding the ticket collector. He managed to do this with great ease. He already had a plan in his mind. When he got off the train and approached the ticket collector, he half bungled his turban and pretended to be in extreme discomfort, shouting to the ticket collector asking where the public toilets were. When the ticket collector asked for the ticket, he shouted at him in no uncertain words saying, is this all that you are bothered about and brushed past him with a nudge. Having gone past the ticket collector, he then straightened his turban and went on his way rejoicing. Great uncle Avtar was a great walker, he could walk for miles and miles considering his age. He was quite a strong and odd character.

Following this lengthy and tedious journey, we eventually arrived in New Delhi and stayed there for about three days. As we were not wealthy enough to stay in a hotel, we stayed at a very large temple. In April, the weather in Delhi was very warm and dry. All of us stayed at the temple and there were hundreds of other people doing the same. You did not have to pay for your accommodation but you just contributed. This is exactly what our family did. This was the custom. We ate some of the meals at the Sikh temple where the meals provided were free. I remember sleeping there on the floor. Before this, I remember going down several steps leading to a pool and immersing myself completely in that refreshing water. This is what most people did. Having come out of the water, I tried to locate my family as several hundred people were sitting there as well as some of them lying on the floor. I eventually managed to find my family who was also split up from one another. So, we spent the night sleeping on the floor at the Sikh Temple. We had a sheet on the floor and a sheet cover. All night tossing and turning with people coming and going and moving about. At least we had somewhere to stay and it was reasonably safe even though we had to watch our belongings all the time.

This temple order also operated a left baggage system, on the condition that the bag or the suitcase had to be locked, so that the temple staff could not be blamed if anything went missing. However, one of the bags belonging to our family did not have a lock on it and the temple staff would not accept it, however hard we tried to persuade them to do so. This disagreement led to an altercation between our great uncle Avtar, and the Temple staff.

Not sure who won the argument. However, having those few days before catching our flight was nice and relaxing but at the same time quite distressing knowing we would be leaving the security of the family we knew and also not knowing what the future would hold. During our stay in Delhi, our family took the opportunity for sightseeing in the great capital knowing we would not have this opportunity again and even if we did, it would not be for some years. This was enjoyable and I can recall sitting on a rickshaw and visiting the Red Fort. It was quite a daunting sight. On our return from seeing all the wonders of New Delhi, except the Taj Mahal, we must have gone out somewhere to eat. The sleeping arrangements were quite loose. We slept on the flat roof of one of the Sikh Temple buildings again. Having seen some of the sights we were also exhausted.

The following day, which I think was also our departing day, we were saying our final goodbyes and shedding some genuine tears. Both families were accompanied to a big office in New Delhi, where there was a good deal of pushing and shoving going on and a handful of papers being exchanged through a small hatch in the window. I had no idea what was going on but I am now fully aware, that this must have been the check-in office for our flight to England. I remember overhearing a part of the conversation that not all of us, meaning the family members who were accompanying us, could go on the same bus to the airport, which was located several miles away from the check-in point. Non-flight passengers had to find their own way to the airport. Having boarded the airport bus, we eventually arrived at the New Delhi International airport. The airport was quite small with very little security around and everything was in the open. At the airport, our family and our neighbour's family, including nonpassengers for the flight went through few doors, produced documents as requested and then all of us came to a small concrete concord, from where we could see the one and only airplane in our sight, which must have been about thirty yards away. We had seen these airplanes in the sky, way above our heads previously but never one as close as that. My heart was beating faster and faster by the second knowing that there is now no turning back. No second thoughts. Democlease's sword was now hanging over our heads and there was no turning back. We must go through what we have to go through. We stood still in silence and no words could express theirs or our feelings. There was no time to be emotional. This was now the time to say thanks to our uncle who had looked after us for many years and had brought us up as his children. There he was standing alongside our great uncle Avtar. It was difficult and sad to say goodbye to everyone. Our uncle gave us the nod to board the plane and the two families stepped off the concord and slowly walked the thirty yards to take our seats for the unknown which would have an impact on our future lives. Uncertainty followed uncertainty, followed by perplexity and puzzlement.

We slowly meandered towards the airplane, looking back but at the same time not looking back. We took our steps forward in anticipation. The feeling of apprehension, doubt, uncertainty, and sadness clung like thick smog you would experience early mornings in London in the sixties. There was now no escape. What could we do? What could we say as we traced and marked each step which took us to the entrance door and we boarded the plane? This was the day we had been waiting for now for several months and years and it had finally arrived like the dawning of another day. What is there to fear but the fear itself except, the fear of the unknown? There was no turning back. This was it. The day had arrived and the goodbyes had been said. I boarded the airplane, step by step using the hard steel step ladder with wheels at the bottom which had been put in place and secured. This was a completely new experience for all of us as a family.

I have never entered a contraption similar to this before. It was a unique experience for me. From the inside, it seemed like an elongated tin of sardines, not that I knew what a tin of sardines looked like it then. The seats were in rows with an aisle in the middle just about wide enough for you to walk sideways. Everything looked quite neat and tidy and even luxurious, not that I was used to luxury and I had nothing to compare it with. It was overwhelming and my emotions were running high. Within minutes of boarding the plane, the stewardess came and helped us to put on the seatbelts and to ensure that we were alright. Then this was followed by another stewardess within seconds bringing some sweets in a bowl for us to choose one or two, to suck during the takeoff. I was wondering if the whole contraption would get up into the sky and if it did would it stay there? The take-off was quite a nerve racking experience, especially, as I did not know what to expect. The airplane would climb up and would then suddenly drop down several hundred feet. It would go up again and would drop down again playing havoc with my stomach. This carried on for some time. Anyway, we were up there and the first leg of the flight stop was to Pakistan, Karachi. This flight was to last for about three hours and my stomach was curling and I was feeling sick. My stomach was not the only stomach upset, so, I have no reason to complain. We took off again from Karachi and the next stop was somewhere in Italy but where in Italy, I have no idea. We were too young to understand where we were and I do not recall doing geography in school. We could be anywhere. Again we stayed at the Italian airport for a short while and there I experienced my first fizzy drink. I enjoyed this a great deal and sucking the liquid through a straw was also a new experience. It's just amazing how minor experiences such as drinking through a straw could be remembered for a lifetime. Not sure what we were doing but just did what other people did. Fantastic experience. In Italy, I recall someone saying they were not sure what to do next, but we will stay close to another family and follow them. They seemed to have a better understanding of what was happening. I suppose, going back almost sixty years ago, people did not travel a great deal and it was a lot easier for the airlines to find their passengers for the next leg of the flight. The airports were quite small and there were not many passengers to monitor. After this stop, we took off again and a few hours later we approached Paris in France. This would be our penultimate stop. The final part of the journey was from Paris to London Heathrow. The journey across the channel was extremely rough. The plane was shaking, vibrating, and wobbling all over the place. How it kept itself together was a miracle in itself. I remember being quite frightened because I was trying to sort out in my mind what was normal and what was not. To me what seemed against all odds, we eventually landed at Heathrow airport, London toward the latter part of the day on 4th April 1960. We were here. We had arrived.

At the airport, we were met by the respective fathers of both of the families. I had no idea who my Dad was, as there were about four men who came to meet and greet us at the airport. We were stunned by what we were experiencing. Everything was so different and not sure what the next step was. I didn't care; we had arrived after a long and tiring flight. We were now safe and with our families. There were no hellos or handshakes etc. and I do not even recall Dad speaking to me. We just followed these odd fellows, who met us and we left them to handle the luggage, not that we brought with us a great deal. The suitcases were almost empty. What could we bring, except one or two rajaies, handmade woolen quilts? At the airport, this was the first time we saw an escalator. It was constantly moving and we were fascinated by it. We had no idea what it was and I eventually put my foot on the step and managed to go up. This was great and I asked my sister Baljinder to try it, but she wouldn't. She described the escalators by saying that the "upstairs was coming down" in Punjabi. I remember this phrase as it seemed very unusual.

By the time both families came out of the airport, it was dark and we all followed to a small minibus or a van. I can recall sitting cramped like a sardine in a tin but we were safe. We were all extremely tired but happy. It was a mixed feeling of apprehension and uncertainty. We were glad that we had arrived safely and soon we would be in our new home. There would be no longer anything to worry about. I suppose there was a feeling of even greater relief that the journey was almost over and it was no longer the ladies responsibility but the men's to make sure that we arrived safely at our new abode. They could now leave it up to them. The ladies had completed their task well.

Having boarded the minibus, we left the airport and travelled on the M1 motorway for the journey. Harban Singh was the owner of the minibus as well as the driver. On the way back, the minibus stopped several times for the men to use the toilet on the hard shoulder. It transpired years later that the men were not stopping to use the non-existent facilities on the hard shoulder, but they were having a swig of whisky or brandy, or even consuming other forms of alcohol. Whatever they had brought with them they consumed. With the undesired additional stops, the journey seemed to be infinite. We eventually arrived at our destination of 339 Newhampton Road West, Wolverhampton in the middle of the night. Of course, we were expected during the night, but whoever opened the door still kept us waiting outside, whilst they were finding a bottle of oil to pour on the door frame and the corner of the steps. This being done we entered the house and a new era in our life had begun. An era that would bring new expectations, joys, sadness, worries, and thrills. They certainly did and they continue to do so even today.

Chapter 8

Settling in England

Waking up on the first morning of our new and permanent home was very strange, not knowing what we were doing or supposed to be doing. I remember it being so, so, so cold. It was the first week in April, with the frost covering the sash windows and the wind howling and biting through the ever-increasing gaps in the windows and doors. These gaps were permanent. It was quite early in the morning and I waited for the sun to rise and give its little ray. All I remember was being cold and shivering. The fire was being lit and soon it would thaw the ice and the frost from the windows, but downstairs only, as the door to the upstairs was kept shut. Soon, we were huddling together by the fire and Dad started to make the chai which was most welcomed. Soon some kind of breakfast would be made. I do not recall what we had for breakfast but there again Mum would not be familiar with using the gas cooker and how to make it come alive by lighting it with a small packet of England's Glory matches. The house was now coming to life with all of us being there and fighting for our little corner in front of the fire. By now the sun had shown its face and we were able to go out for a brief time, rubbing our hands and warming them with our breath. Life now took on a new meaning as we began to settle little by little into this strange and unknown world. I was grateful that our two families were living together, as there is strength in numbers regardless of our little bickering from time to time amongst us as kids. It's strange how you begin to appreciate each other even though you fight for your little corner from time to time.

I discovered in the morning that the house which our two families now occupied together was a three-bedroom old terrace house situated on the main road on Newhampton Road West, Whitmoreans, Wolverhampton. There was no hallway and you entered the house straight into the lounge from the pavement. Downstairs the accommodation consisted of a lounge, which we called the front room. As you entered the house, on the right-hand side was a small coal fire with a four-inch tiled fireplace with some of the tiles chipped. It looked very nice and the coal fire was the essential part of the room without which it would be difficult to survive. It had a carpet on the floor; wallpapered walls and a picture hanging rail approximately two feet below the ceiling. This room led straight into the dining room which also had a coal fire similar to the one in the lounge. From the dining room, you could enter a small and elongated kitchen which had an old-fashioned white sink with two taps firmly fixed on it. Looking hind side, the kitchen was outdated but it did its job. This was luxury compared to our facilities in Jandiala. The whole experience was very strange as we were used to going to the well or to the water pump to fetch the water. How could this be? How does the water get here? Although there was one tap marked hot water, we never used this, as we did not have hot water in the house because the immersion was never put on except on Saturdays. After all, that was a bath day. The bathroom was added to the house at a later date. There was an outside door in the kitchen that led to a small paved backyard and from which you accessed the toilet, the coal house, and the small back garden. The toilet room was very cold and there was no electric light in it and the wooden locking door was about four inches short at the base and also at the top of the door frame. You could access the upstairs from the dining room by steep stairs, which led to three bedrooms. At the top of the stairs, on the left, was the front bedroom which was of a reasonable size, and on the right were two further bedrooms. The first one was of a reasonable size and from which you accessed the third small elongated room. You could not access the third bedroom without going into the second bedroom. However, this is not a complaint of the living condition but a reality of how we survived.

Would you believe that both families shared this small three-bedroom terrace house? Our family consisted of three boys and two girls and mum and dad. The second family consisted of one boy and a girl as well as their parents. Thus making a total of eleven people including teenagers. The other family had their bedrooms and we had ours. The sleeping arrangements were very tight. Our family of three boys occupied the second bedroom and our sisters occupied the small box room. Mum and dad initially slept downstairs in the front room. The other family occupied the front bedroom and I cannot recall where the girl slept but the boy also shared the boy's bedroom. I have not yet mentioned that from time to time we also had guests staying with us. It was difficult but we managed. Our Dad and Tarsam's Dad, Resham Singh, brought this terraced house together for six hundred pounds in 1960 or it may have been in 1959. This was the only way that our two families could afford to have somewhere for us to live and also to pay for their families to come to England. These times were very hard and we were not the only family in this situation. This was almost the norm, how the majority of the people lived in that era. After several months, the second family moved into a council house at Portobello Road, Willenhall on the outskirts of Wolverhampton. We were very friendly with this family and we would see them frequently at the weekends.

As I recounted earlier on, times were hard and the winter always got to us. I recall that on one occasion, a Thursday evening, we had run out of coal. This was the last thing that we should have done because this was the only means of heating the house. There was no such thing as central heating. Although there were fireplaces in the bedrooms, these were never lit except on a very rare occasion. The coal lorry would call regularly in the area and from time to time we would store this black commodity in the coal bunker next to the outside toilet. There were two fireplaces, one in the front room and the second one in the dining room. We did not always light the fire in the front room but would light the fire in the dining room. This dining room was like a thoroughfare and the heat would escape to other parts of the house. We would just hug the fire in the evening and then go off to bed. Almost every night, we would put our heads under the rajai and would hope to warm up very quickly. However, on this Thursday there was no coal in the coal bunker and there was no money either until dad would get his weekly pay packet on Friday evening. On several previous occasions, I have been with Dad to the coal yard which was at five ways, Whitmoreans in Wolverhampton which was about half a mile away from where we lived. We would go in and ask the owner for a bag of coal, which he would then weigh on the big massive red Avery scales which we would then carry home either using a wheelbarrow or on our shoulders. On this particular occasion, I remember going to the coal yard with Dad on a Saturday morning very early and waiting with others for the coal yard to open. I was just standing there, wearing a royal blue school blazer but no overcoat as I did not have one and every part of my body frozen. The clock ticking as slowly as it could and the time standing still. The flurry of snow stopping and starting every few minutes. It seemed centuries and then there was a minute noise of footsteps crackling in the frost and the frozen snow from the freezing night temperature. Yes, the coal merchant had come to life and then I heard the clink of the padlock being removed from the inside of the big wooden gates. There was still life left in us as all of us were rubbing our hands together. Dad and I were the second or the third customer to be served as Dad did the transaction and handed over the money. With chattering teeth and my whole body shivering, I waited patiently for the merchant to start weighing the coal on the scales and unload them into the wheelbarrow. With frozen bare hands, I wheeled the barrow home stopping from time to time to warm my hands as they were sticking to the wheelbarrow handles. About three houses away from our house was the alley which ran along the side of our neighbour's houses and their gardens which gave access to our back garden and our coal bunker. Having dumped the coal in the bunker and taking some of the coal inside to the dining area, I then walked back immediately to the coal merchant's yard to return the wheelbarrow so that other customers could use it. To us, this was nothing unusual and we would wait for the next occasion.

Another one of our weekly rituals was taking a weekly bath. Our small terrace house did not have a bathroom except for the outside toilet. Every Saturday morning, some of us would get up and following breakfast would walk to the local community baths which were located on Bath Road opposite the local Tax office. It was an old building and as you entered it you would smell the odour of chlorinated atmosphere but it was warm. Located on the right hand side were the baths and on the left hand side was a large swimming pool of a depth of seven feet. There was also a smaller pool on the right hand side which was mainly used for swimming lessons with small cubicles along its side, which were used as changing rooms. Not only that but there was also a communal changing room on the balcony upstairs.

As you entered the building you had to purchase a ticket, indicating if you were there for swimming or taking a bath. We were there to take our baths as this was our custom. These baths were housed in a large cubicle and overseen by ladies who would clean the baths for the next customer. In the meantime, you just had to wait in the queue and you never knew how long it would be before your turn. You would fill the bath with the water as you got changed, controlled your water temperature, and so on. There was a wooden chair in the cubicle for you to put your clothes on. Having taken your bath, you would pull the old large plastic plug for the dirty water to go down. Some of the Asian ladies were taking quite a long time in taking their baths and holding others up. It transpired later, that they were not only taking their bath as they were supposed to, but also doing their laundry. They would empty the bath and then refill it again for their laundry. No wonder they were taking a long time. The council became aware of this and they then changed the routine. From then on, only the ladies supervising the baths were allowed to clean and refill the baths with hot water. Once this has been done, they would then call the next customer. What a cheek. In no way you could refill it and do your laundry. What an Indian reputation.

Chapter 9

Culture Vulture

On our first few days of arriving in England, being thrust into a different culture was a shock and it was very strange. It looked very odd at the time, as I could not see crowds and crowds of people out on the streets going about their daily lives, men wearing a turban and ladies in salwar and kameez and none of them riding their bikes. It was cold on April 5th, 1960 in Wolverhampton. The sun was not shining, except momentarily and certainly not giving the warmth of the day as it did in India. First thing in the morning, it seemed all foggy, so the visibility was quite poor as you looked down the road. Looking outside was very strange and eerie. Just a few cars were going up and down the road. We dare not venture out. It was scary and it gave you a feeling of uncertainty, apprehensiveness, and confusion. No cows in the street, no cow pats, no one running or shouting. Our house had glass in the windows, there were carpets on the floor as well as a couple of pictures hanging on the wall. As we looked outside again, men had short hair and white, pale skin. Women were in skirts you could see their legs, strangely dressed but clean and smart, long hair of various colours, blond, ginger, black and so on. Tarmac roads, people in cars rushing to work first thing in the morning, people shivering and rubbing their hands together to keep warm. Most of the people were wearing long thick coats, hats, and woolen grey or black gloves. People hopping on and off the trolleybuses whilst the bus was still moving. This was quite a common practice as the back end of the bus on the pavement side was an open platform area for people to get on and off the bus. At times, we would jump on the bus as it was accelerating to avoid missing it altogether. There were no such issues as health and safety guidelines as there are now. When it was very frosty and cold, the contact bars on the trolleybuses would generate sparks and the contact bars would quite often come off the electric cables. The conductor or the bus driver would then get off the bus, using a long wooden pole; he would try to put the contact bars on the electric cables again. This was more difficult as the bus tried to go round the corner or around the bend in the road. The front doors on the trolleybuses were always shut and the conductor would let you on and off the bus. He had a little ticket machine that worked on cogwheels and he would issue small tickets of various colours depending upon how your fare was made up. There were no lady drivers or conductors. All this came a bit later. The conductor would say "Hold tight please" as the bus would move. I remember walking past the bus station in India. There were only two buses and they did not seem to be going anywhere. The driver tried to start the bus but could not. The fuel of the bus was probably diesel. There were about four men gathered around the bus but it would not start. I then saw one of the men setting fire to a dirty oily rag and then putting it under the engine compartment. I suppose this is where the fuel tank was. It seemed that they had to warm up the diesel for it to flow. The viscosity of the Diesel in those days used to be like that of treacle. How our resources have changed over the past years.

In India, in our village, the doors of our houses were rarely shut except in the evening when it was getting dark or during the inclement weather. In England, the doors were always shut. All this seemed very strange, unfamiliar, and out of routine. There were proper pavements and you could walk or run on without the risk of tripping over a protruding object or holes and craters in your path. No dogs roaming the streets and barking or even turning up at your door begging for food. There was no one patrolling the streets at night and shouting for the thieves to leave, "Beware I am here". The streets were lit so that you could go out in the dark. The shops would close around five in the evening and also on Wednesday afternoons, and every Sunday, yet the shops in our bazaar in India would stay open till ten at night. The English shops were very clean and well kept. There were proper scales to measure the weights of goods. We just take these things for granted. The shops displayed odd things in the windows which were unfamiliar to us at the time but we got the hang of it quite quickly especially when it came to sweets. We would buy boiled sweets, arrow toffees, myty which was like rice crispies covered in chocolate, penny sweets and so on.

We had Indian neighbours. When I say neighbours they lived seven doors away from our little three-bed room terraced house. These houses are no longer there. They have been demolished and new ones built. New houses are also terrace houses but they are new build and very modern. This neighbouring family came over from Ludhiana, in Punjab. I think they came about eighteen months before our family arriving. Their family arrangements were very, very strange which I didn't understand at the time. They were well off financially because they seemed to have everything going for them. They had a radio and a TV, whereas we had none of these luxuries. I would spend a considerable amount of time at their house between coming home from school and the six o'clock news on BBC1. Their mother whose name was Balbinder Kaur was living with her son Narinder Singh alone. She also had another son, Gurbachan Singh, who did not live with them at home but came home from time to time. There was a rift between him and his father Mr. C who had committed polygamy, as he was also married to an English lady and together they lived in Bilston near Wolverhampton. Through this polygamy, they had two daughters. No one dared to challenge him or his position. He was big and obese. Almost every midweek day at lunchtime, he would come to see his Indian wife who would cook for him and his two or three minders, whom he would bring with him. They would stay for about an hour and after lunch, he would go, together with his minders until the following day. This was his routine. I would not be able to trust him. His Indian wife was afraid of him in case she got evicted following any disagreement with him. The problem was, that she was not familiar with the laws of this land and secondly she was completely illiterate and therefore helpless. She had no choice but to put up with him and his minders. Narinder and I got on well with each other. As Narinder had been here longer, his spoken and written language was better than mine. He was a homely person with a lot of confidence knowing that he would be well looked after. He had the opportunity to go on school outings and holidays. I remember him talking all about it and doing his logbook for the school which was neat and included some photographs following his school trip to Capel Curig.

Mr. C came over from Ludhiana to England in the early fifties alone and soon established himself as a businessman. He had all the acumens of a business person. Soon after his arrival to the UK, he was struggling to find suitable work as he was unwilling to do manual work, where you would get your hands dirty. This was nothing unusual as there were others in the same position. However, soon after his arrival, he borrowed money from his friends, promising to pay them back as soon as he could. There was nothing unusual about that either. With the borrowed money he purchased a cheap house in a cheap area for his use as well as renting some of the rooms to his friends. At that time, the Asian people who were coming to the UK had very little financial security or familiarity with the culture. The first and second generation of immigrants were mainly illiterate and had very little command of the English language. Mr. C was very happy to take advantage of them by giving them a helping hand as long as it suited him. This brought him a good income. He then used the rental income to buy another property which he again rented out to whoever was desperate to rent.

Mr. C accelerated his business by buying old properties which were in dire need of repair, had been on the market for a considerable amount of time or the vendors were desperate to sell. He would buy these properties at a very, very low price, and then he would repair them as cheaply as he could. He would then sell them to the people who were finding it difficult to get a mortgage. In the process, he employed painters, decorators, bricklayers, carpenters, and so on. Not only that he had some contacts with mortgage companies, conveyancing people, and so on. In the midst of all that, he also started his own finance company where he would lend the deposit to the buyers, as long as they brought the houses that he was selling. The interest rates would be extortionate. If people did not pay, he had his minders to deal with them. If you look around in the Wolverhampton, Bilston, and the Willenhall area, you will come across some of the houses where the bricks are painted red. This was his emblem. So, you could tell immediately which houses he was involved in.

When we came to England, as a family we were all of the Sikh religion. I had long hair and the length of my hair came almost halfway down my back. It was normal for me to wear a turban which I had done every day in India. After few days of being in England, Dad took Satvant and Gurnam to the barber to have their hair cut short. Both Satvant and Gurnam did but I refused point-blank. I felt so insecure without my hair and turban. However, this lasted only for another week or so and it was soon sorted out following our second visit to the barber. It was so strange hearing the noise of the clippers and someone pushing and pulling your hair. I was wondering what I would look like. I could now feel the wind and the cold on my head. It was painful and I felt as if I was not dressed properly. It was such a strange feeling and a culture shock.

Going to school for the first time in Wolverhampton was quite scary. Except for Gurnam and Baljinder, we were registered at Whitmoreans Secondary Modern School on Hordern Road in the area of Whitmoreans in Wolverhampton. As none of us could converse or understand English, the administration task was done by Lucy Price. She was a wonderful lady and nothing seemed to be any trouble for her. She lived about two miles away from where we lived, yet she would walk faithfully as many times as necessary to sort out our numerous administrative tasks that had to be done, as well as our family problems. Wherever and whenever the paperwork was involved, she was there. She was very competent and faithful in all that she did. She was engaged to be married to Harbans Singh. She lived on Upper Zoar Street. In the local community where she lived, she had an excellent reputation and everything she did was above reproach. She was a very honest and caring young lady. She sorted out our school registration and took us to school on our first day.

Within a few days of arriving in England, we were on our way to school. Going to an English school was strange. The school was within a walking distance of where we lived and it took us about ten minutes to get there. We were able to come home for lunch each day which was a big bonus for us as children because we were not familiar with English food. This was also a bonus for our parents as they did not have to pay for school lunches. In addition to this, was the problem of being able to use a knife and a fork, which did not come naturally to us. It seems a simple task if you have been brought up with it from birth, but not if you are thrust into an unfamiliar situation where you already feel very vulnerable and insecure. Your hands, fingers, eyes, and spatial coordination had to be learned, especially when it came to eating peas. Thankfully, I never had school dinners.

On our first day, we were taken to school by Lucy Price. She had to take Gurnam and Baljinder, the younger ones first and when this task had been completed it was our turn. We walked in through the front gates and she took us to the Head Master's office. From there we were told which classes we would be in. By the time this was done, it was break time and during that time we were introduced to some other Indian children so that we would feel at home. At that time in this school, there could not have been more than about eight other Indian children and about five West Indian children. We made friends with the Indian boys quite quickly. I was placed in the "D" stream of the first year. This was the lowest they could put me into due to not being able to communicate in English. For the following academic year, I was kept in the D stream of the first year. The following year I moved into the "D" stream of the second year and then into the "C" stream. Through sheer hard work, I ended up in the A stream of the fourth year in the last academic term. As I was only there for one term, my exam results were not brilliant as I did not have the opportunity to complete the other academic work. I was very pleased with my achievement. I enjoyed my school days. As with most kids, you have good days and not-so-good days but they were fun days and I have good memories of that.

As I mentioned earlier, I moved from the "D" stream to the "A" stream within three years. This incident takes me back to when I was moved from a "3D" class to the "3C" class at the end of a term. When I started in "3C", Mr. Lewis was the woodwork teacher. He was very old-fashioned in his ways. He would stop the whole of the class to explain something if someone was not doing it properly. I think this incident must have been in my first week of being in his class. The class was doing their examination in Technical Drawing. Never mind doing the exam, I had not even heard of Technical Drawing or what it meant. I had no idea where to start. It so happened that I was sitting next to Peter Price, a classmate. Mr. Lewis came over as I had no idea what to do, so he asked Peter Price to do my drawing as well as his. Two weeks later on, having marked the examination papers, it transpired that I had more marks than Peter Price. He was not happy. I was not aware of it at the time, but I later discovered that Mr. Lewis was also a Christian and he was also on the Methodist list of circuit preachers. I came across this information whilst I was in Church one Sunday morning at Lord Street Methodist Church. Being a Methodist Church, different preachers came to take the morning and evening services. Surprise, surprise, Mr. Lewis came to take the morning service. I was so pleased to see him and wondered if it was truly him. How could this be? Following the service, he and I had a good natter. After that, I was always the favourite in his class and I could not put a foot wrong. He would treat me very well which I thoroughly enjoyed.

One thing that I never enjoyed at school was sport because I was never any good at it. On coming to England, I had problems with my knee joints. They would just give way and when this happened, they were very painful. Having not been in this country long, I approached my GP to see what the problem was but he could not diagnose it. However, eventually, I was referred to what I think now was the Physiotherapy Department. To strengthen my knee joints, I was wired up and connected to a machine that sent electrical signals across my knees. It was similar to having small electrical shocks across my joints. The modern version of that is, that I was connected to a TENS machine. I went and had this treatment for several weeks. I don't think it made a great deal of difference. In contrast, whilst I was in India, I had no problems with my knee joints. There was also another lad who had a problem with his health. Both of us would be amongst the last to come in a cross country race which I always hated. We would always be the last to be picked in the teams. As I never enjoyed sport, I would have been very happy not to take part in any, except that it was obligatory. On another occasion, it was lunchtime from school and I had to go for something towards Hunter Street from home. As I was walking on the pavement, I recognised another pupil from the school coming towards me. As I walked toward him, I could sense some trouble coming. He saw me and I saw him. I became aware that he was going to attack me. So as we approached each other, I was fully prepared for him. As we approached, he went for me with his fists without a word being spoken, which he missed. Soon we were both rolling about on the pavement punching each other. Fortunately, he came off worse than I did. Soon we were both at school for our afternoon classes. He had spread the word that I had beaten him at lunchtime for no apparent reason. Another friend of mine at school told me that I must rush home from school as he and his mates were going to beat me up on the way home. After school, on the way home, the bully and his friends did chase me and punched me few times. The following day, I was escorted by I think it was Resham Singh, who then had a word with the Headmistress. No one touched me or bullied me ever again knowing that if they did I would beat them up one to one. The lad who fought me was quite a tough guy.

I also enjoyed religious studies at school. At school, as part of the teaching programme, we were to learn about different denominations, so ministers from different denominations were invited to come and inform us of the denominational differences. As I had been involved in Methodism, there is no reason why our Minister Rev. D N Howarth should not come and talk to us. So, with this in view, I approached our Religious studies teacher and he was very positive about my involvement. So, I organized his visit which I thought went extremely well.

At the time of coming to England, I could not speak a word of English. English was on the school curriculum in Jandiala from class six on upward; I had no teaching in English. Communication was a major issue that had to be overcome. The first few words that I learned in English were "I do not understand you and I do not speak English". The school was very good to us as a family. We were often pulled out of our normal lessons and given English tuition individually or with another family member and we would also do our homework. This was often done in a fun way. We would play lexicon, cards, puzzles, crosswords, and so on. Formal education soon came to an end in July 1963. As a result of that, I missed out on subjects such as geography, history, art, etc. These subjects have always been of less importance to me as I do not have the foundation on these subjects.

It was customary, that before you left school, you had a career interview with the Careers Officer who visited the school. I was now in my final year at school. Just before leaving school, I had a three-minute interview with the Careers Advisor. Career advice was offered to all school leavers as a routine but it did not mean anything. As we were at a Secondary Modern School, we were seen as being employed as blue-collar workers. In other words, being employed in a non-professional capacity. We would work as labourers, manual factory workers, milkmen, car mechanics, or anything to do with our hands as we would not be intelligent enough to pursue a professional career. The Career Advisor asked, what was my father employed as? I said that he was working as a labourer. The Career Advisor's advice was to go and do likewise. I don't recall him saying anything much more than that. However, Dad had other plans for us and he wanted us to embark on a new and exciting adventure and train as car mechanics. This would be his pinnacle of achievement for Satvant and me. Then we could have our own business by opening a garage and do the repair and maintenance work on the cars. Having listened to various people, I decided to go to college for a year to study General Engineering. I applied to the college and they called me up to do a written test before they could consider offering me a place on this course. The topic was to debate the argument for and against "Corporal Punishment". So, I set about writing and I later discovered that I was writing about "Capital Punishment" instead. Regardless of my error, I managed to get a place at Wulfrun College of Further Education in Wolverhampton which was within a walking distance of home. I was going to study General Engineering for one year. This was quite nice and I enjoyed it. Whilst there I made several good friends.

Let me go back to the subject of Technical Drawing again. As part of the Engineering course, Technical Drawing was a major part of the course and we had to embrace it fully. Our lecturer for this subject was Mr. Rose who was a stocky fellow with daring eyes and the sort of person you don't want to cross. Discipline followed by more discipline was his utmost attitude. He was very old-fashioned in his thinking and his character. He wore a white nylon overcoat so that he would not get any chalk on his clothes. We had Technical Drawing on a Monday afternoon. We had to be in before the lesson was to commence and as soon as he entered the classroom, all the students had to stand up behind their desks. No exceptions. He would say "Good afternoon class" and we would have to reply "Good afternoon Mr. Rose". There would be no talking and he would set up what he wanted us to do. He explained what he wanted us to do. If for any reason we wanted to leave the room, we would have to put our hand up and then seek his permission which was not always granted. Mid-afternoon tea breaks were finished early, as there would be a punishment of some kind if you were late returning. On one occasion, he set us homework which was quite difficult to do and seemed to be beyond our capabilities. So, hardly anyone did it except for about two people in the class. On the morning of Mr. Rose's lesson, the homework was printed by these lads and handed to most of the students. All we had to do was to put our name on the copied paper and hand it in which we all did. Even though the answers were correct, we were given a zero mark which we would have had as if we had not done it.

I can recall another incident, which I am not sure if it took place in the first year or the second year of my Engineering course. The subject was Engineering Science. The lecturer's name was Mr. Price. I am sure he knew his subject well but he just could not put it over to the students, however hard he tried. Therefore, he could not control his class and none of us would pay a great deal of attention to his teaching. At break times, some of the students would make sure that they came in late and some would be even later to ensure that the whole class would be disturbed. After few weeks, Mr. Price almost lost his temper with the class saying, that he has had enough of this type of behaviour and he was no longer going to tolerate it. If we came in late next time, we would find our chair and our books outside the room and we would not be allowed to enter the classroom. So, after the break, all of us came in on time and we all behaved well. However, the following week Mr. Price was late. So, two of the students picked up his chair, including his papers and the class register, and put it outside the class. A few minutes later, Mr. Price walked in carrying his chair and his papers. You should have seen the expression on his face.

Toward the end of this course, all the students were looking for work or indentured apprenticeships. It was very competitive. To get some sort of an apprenticeship was quite an achievement, especially if you went to a Secondary Modern School. To get an apprenticeship, I applied to several companies engaged in the engineering industry but without success. As students, we exchanged lots of information between ourselves but I was not that successful in my applications. I later discovered the problem. Nine of the students applied to James Gibbons Ltd, which was a local engineering company in Wolverhampton for an apprenticeship. There were six white English students and three Asian/black students. All six white English students were offered the apprenticeship but not the remainder. This discrimination was so obvious. This was not the only company who were discriminating against non-English people. When it became so obvious of the discriminatory practices, I dropped my middle name "Singh" and I would sign the application letters as Jagir Kalu. Having done that, I was then being offered interviews but still not selected. I was looking for a student apprenticeship. Student apprenticeship was almost a guarantee for an office job. After several applications and interviews, I was offered a Craft Apprenticeship at Chubb and Sons, Lock and Safe Co Ltd. This was not what I wanted to do but had to accept, as there were no alternative offers. I then started my apprenticeship in August 1964 and completed it in August 1969. For the first few months, we were doing very basic tasks such as filing, sawing, measuring and how to use the equipment correctly, and so on. After few months we were thrown onto the shop floor where we worked under supervision. We spent three months at a time in different departments. I enjoyed being there. Whilst there, George was one of the foremen and he was in his early sixties at the time. He was a great and very helpful guy and he was respected by all. His attitude was very positive. One of the many jobs that I had to do for him every lunchtime was to leave early and go to the pub which was on the corner of Woden Road, off Wednesfield Road and get him two cheese and onion cobs or two ham cobs. This was quite nice, as I could go and wash my hands early before the crowd left for their lunch and get ready to fetch his lunch. In case I was late returning from my lunch, he would sign my clocking-in card.

Towards the end of my apprenticeship, there were several disagreements between the shop floor management and the office management as to who should finance my final two years part-time or six months block release studies. The issue was, if I should pass the final stage, I would end up in the offices and if I failed I would belong on the shop floor. Who was to know if I was going to pass or not. Therefore, no one was interested. I was not offered block release, so I had to study part-time for the first year. As I had completed and passed the first year, unlike some of those on block release, I was finally offered a block release in the second year which I passed with flying colours.

I started on the shop floor and I ended up as one of their Design Engineers. Whilst there, I led the company into Metrication as this was seen as the future. Part of my remit was to advise the company management and the design engineers on future product design materials, sizes, and consumable products, such as screws, nuts, bolts, the thickness of materials, etc. This was an integral part of standardisation and rationalisation. This new role was quite exciting as I was the only one in this position, until one day when they appointed a new Managing Director. Within days of the new management being appointed, we came into work one Monday morning to find all our desks had been moved and we had been given new positions and my Metrication department disbanded. I soon left the company in 1973, as the atmosphere at work was not conducive. I was not the only one who left Chubb and Sons, as several others were unhappy at work. My manager, Neil C, was the second Chief Engineer whose desk had been moved into a side corner office. He was very frightened of what was going to happen to him, because every time his phone rang, he shook and stuttered.

I acquired a new post within days with John A Smith, Design Consultants in 1973, just off the Dudley Road in Wolverhampton. Having started this new job on a Monday, I was told by the Shop Steward on the same afternoon that we were all out on strike tomorrow morning due to a breakdown in pay negotiations. There was no choice but to go out with the rest. Whilst working there, I did some design work on the Concorde which I shall never forget. There was so much guidance on how the design had to be done.

There was guidance on which type of lead pencil should be used for drawing the outline, detail drawing, lettering, height, and the spacing of the letters. It was time consuming with very little progress. Whilst working as a Design Engineer, my eyes began to take the strain and I felt that I needed to have a career change. I left this company in 1977 to train as an Instrument Engineer. This training was TOPS training in Wrexham to where I was commuting every morning from Shrewsbury.

John A Smith being a Design Consultant company acquired several contracts locally and nationally. One of these contracts was with GEC, an Engineering Company based in Stafford. I was asked, together with another Engineer, if I was interested in that contract to which my response was affirmative. The other Engineer lived about ten miles nearer to Stafford than I did. So, every morning I would make my way to his house and then we would travel together. It worked out fine until one day my moped broke down on the return journey. I had to abandon the moped and catch the bus home. It so happened, the moped was picked up by the police who contacted me to come and pick it up. I turned up to pick up the moped from the Police Station, but I did not have my helmet with me. As I picked up the moped, I checked at the Police Station to see if I can pedal it and they said, as long as you pedal it and not have the engine running, I would be fine, as it only acts like a bicycle. So, all was fine. I was pedalling it on Waterloo Road in Wolverhampton and as I approached the Molineux Football ground, I was stopped by a Policeman who questioned me about not wearing a helmet. I explained to him, that I have had permission to ride it as long as I pedalled it. He became quite stroppy and started to check the state of my moped. Whilst all this was going on, another Policeman turned up who supported what the Policeman was saying. Then he threatened to arrest me if I got on that moped without my helmet. As I did not want to be arrested, I had no choice but to push the moped until I reached the centre of Wolverhampton. As I still had about three miles to go, I saw another Policeman and this time I approached him and explained to him the different advice I had been given and asked him for his opinion. He said I suggest that you pedal the moped but go the back way where you will not be picked up. So, that is exactly what I did. It was quite a tiring and annoying day.

Following training in instruments and control loop systems, I later worked as an Engineer at Iron Bridge Power Station from 1978 to 1984, where I decided to change my career again from Engineering to Social Work. However, in between leaving school and starting my apprenticeship a lot happened.

Before I move on to the next chapter, I must share this incident with you. Being financially independent meant that I had full freedom to travel as I wished. I have always enjoyed travelling and still do. In the summer of 1966, which can be remembered as the year when England won the World Football Cup. My friend Trevor E, my brother Satvant and I decided to go camping around Europe. We intended to travel overland to Austria, Switzerland, and Italy. Trevor had an old Ford van which he used for work with no seats in the back. We used this for travelling and carrying our camping equipment. As there were no seats, Trevor improvised by placing a wooden box as a seat in the back. In those days, you could take your car by air abroad and that was exactly what we did. All went well and we landed at Calais airport or near there. As my passport was being checked by the Immigration Department, I was asked to step aside by the Immigration officer and wait, which I did. He checked my passport again and then took me to his office and refused entry. I could not understand why as none of us could understand French. It emerged that as I was the holder of an Indian Passport, I required a visa to enter France and the other countries that we were hoping to travel through. I had to wait in his office and I was deported back to England on the next flight. What a dilemma, what shall I do? Should they go without me? On arrival back to the UK, with little money, I walked for several miles towards London hoping I was going in the right direction. I was eventually picked up by a lorry driver who dropped me off near Dagenham. I know it was Dagenham because I was not far away from the Ford Dagenham factory.

Trying to find overnight accommodation during the World Football Cup was a nightmare and very expensive. I managed to find bed and breakfast for two nights and as soon as I could I made my way to the French, German, Belgium, Austrian, and the Swiss Embassies and managed to get the visas over the two days and then travelled to Luton airport to join the others in France. What a fiasco! On returning home my priority was to be naturalised and apply for British Citizenship which I did and acquired.

Chapter 10

From Sikhism to Seekism

ollowing arrival to England in April 1960, I could not speak a word of English, so instructions such as sit down, lunch time, wait, etc. were unfamiliar to us as a family. Dad decided that we should settle and integrate quickly into the community and stressed to all of us the importance of learning the English language. He further went on to stress that all of this will be to our advantage at a later date. He was spot on. He knew from personal experience that unless we integrated into the community, we would be at a disadvantage all our lives. His encouragement paid off. To enable us to integrate, all of us were encouraged to go to Sunday school every Sunday; integrate into the community and learn from the community. The sole purpose of our attendance at the Lord Street Methodist Church, near Chapel Ash, was to do just that. Heeding his advice, all of us started to attend this Methodist church within three weeks of our arrival in England. We had no idea where this place was, or what they did there. So, we had a lift to church as children in a small open-top sports car owned and driven by Trevor E. He was just a few more years older than us, so, he could drive. He would come religiously every Sunday afternoon to pick us up and all five of us would be squeezed in almost sitting on each other. The space was so tight. We did not mind, it was a car so we did not have to walk. He was also very generous with his time. He loved cars and he was a fully qualified Car Mechanic. All this was well before health and safety and seat belts and MOTs and so on. There were very few cars on the road in the early sixties and public transport was most commonly used.

Going to church was fun and very different from what used to take place in the Gurdwara in our village in Jandiala. We had to get used to singing the choruses in a different language in church, doing the actions, reading and praying, and so on. Lucy Price, who was the Sunday School Superintendant at the time, encouraged us a great deal. She had a tremendous impact on all of our lives. This routine of going to church carried on for several months and then suddenly, we all dropped off going to church except for Satvant and me. This was our parent's wish as they did not want us to be serious about church and Christianity. Following this, our two sisters were no longer allowed to go. Being boys we had a bit more freedom. By then Satvant and I had settled at the church and both of us made very good friends with the people from within the church. We were part of a small group of young people with whom we had a lot of contact and we supported each other and formed good links. Some of these people were Butch, Margaret, Maureen, Pat, Robert, Jim, John, and Pauline. Mr. Bicknall was a regular attendee at Lord Street, he must have been in his sixties and he was still a bachelor. He was a very committed Christian. He was a very short man and he reminded me of Zacchaeus who also was a very small man. He was bald and his head would shine like the morning glory. He would carry his briefcase, umbrella and would wear a black hat. He walked like a city trader. He had a lovely gentle personality. He was indeed a great encouragement to us as he took interest in us, in our family, and our education. However, after several months of attending church, I too dropped off as I was no longer interested in going to church but more interested in playing football in West Park with my mates. I must have been about fourteen at the time. Having been away for several weeks from church, unexpectedly Maureen and Margaret, two of our friends turned up on our doorstep. I went to open the door and there they were. I stood there with my mouth wide open and not knowing what to do or what to say. Completely baffled and taken by surprise. Was I to invite them into the house which I suppose was the decent thing to do? I didn't. I was totally in shock. They were the last people I had expected to turn up on my doorstep. Two lovely white young ladies just turning up to see me. Well, from an Indian cultural point of view this was not the done thing. In the Indian culture boys and girls just did not mix. What are my parents going to say or do? The two cultures had very little to do with each other and not only that, they were English girls which added even more embarrassment. No, I did not invite them in and all I wanted them to do was to disappear immediately without a trace. If my parents knew, what was I going to say to them? As they stood outside our front door on the pavement, they expressed their concern that they were missing me at church and it would be good if I came back. It was quite difficult not knowing how to react. I did not want to be seen with these English girls especially in front of my parents. I just wanted them to disappear, go away, and never to call again. Just to get them away from the doorstep, I promised that I will see them next Sunday and then closing the door immediately. They must have thought that I was really rude having no manners. The whole conversation must have lasted about three minutes. I realized later that they made a great effort to come and see me as they lived about two to three miles away and had used public transport. Later, I regretted my actions and what

I had said. However, following their visit I did go to church the following Sunday and then returned and attended church regularly.

By the time I was about 15 years of age, my English had significantly improved and it seemed to me that there was no personal gain in attending the church regularly. However, regardless of that, I did attend regularly as my friendship with the folks at church became stronger. Also at the same time, both John W and Jim G had started a small house group for the young people on a Friday night. This small group consisted of Satvant, Robert, Maureen, Margaret, and Trevor. We would spend most of the evening playing Monopoly and then finish off with supper and a reading from the Bible and prayer. In hindsight, they were very fruitful years and they had a great impact on my life. Jim and John had left this legacy for the young people, not only by what they did for us but also by their teaching and commitment and by their personal life and testimony.

I recall it was the week before Easter, at the age of 15 years in 1962, I was asked by David L, who was a regular attendee at Lord Street Methodist Church, to come to a special meeting on Good Friday evening. There were other people from the church going too. I was very reluctant to go and felt there was no point in going. It being Good Friday, I could stay in and watch a bit of TV. Instead of saying straight no, I said that if I did not have any other commitment then I would consider it. Lo and behold, I did not have any other commitment or anything else on my agenda, so I decided to go to the meeting. David had already informed me where and what time to meet him. This meeting was to have the greatest impact on my life and it still does even today. Having walked one and a half miles to meet him and then travelling to the meeting together on a cold, wet, and foggy dark evening, we finally reached our destination. We were late for the meeting due to the weather conditions. We had travelled for a considerable amount of time in the car, but I had no idea where we were. On arrival at our destination, we entered an old Methodist chapel and on entering this old chapel, I discovered that it was fully packed with people and there were no seats left. All five of us were guided by the stewards to the front of the church and then to the left where the choir would normally sit. I was on the last seat and the last pew on the right hand side at the back. We all had to budge up. I also noticed that, as I was walking toward the front of the chapel, I saw on the pulpit a blue cloth spread over the electon with the words "Follow Me" written on it. We sang several hymns and then the preacher began to preach and chose the text from the Gospel according to Luke chapter 9 verse 23. I don't recall a great deal of what the preacher preached on or what he had said except for these very words which I saw earlier. "Follow Me". In other words to follow Jesus. What has this to do with me, I thought? I am born and bred as a Sikh, even though I knew a bit about the Bible, having listened to the biblical stories during the past three years. My feet were very cold as there was no heating in the car as we travelled, so my mind was concentrating on getting warm. As the preacher preached, I began to concentrate a bit more as it became more interesting. I was becoming very disturbed during the sermon, which I did not understand a great deal of except for the command to "Follow me". To follow Jesus! My consciousness was now challenging my own life as the preacher was talking about hell and our sinful state, God, being the Judge, and how one day we will have to stand before him. He began to talk about the reason why Jesus came and the ransom he paid on our behalf by shedding his blood on the cross. He rose again from the dead and ascended to heaven. He said and I realised, that our good works or being a devout Sikh will have no impact on the judgment day because we have all sinned. That was the reason why Jesus came to pay the price of our sins. During the meeting, I became slowly aware that God was calling me to repentance from my wicked way and to surrender my life to Jesus. There was a battle going on in my mind as to what I should do. The preacher then made an altar call to which I did not respond. During the alter call, some members of the congregation went forward for counselling and prayers. Anyway, no one knew that I was seeking God's face so what's the problem, so I thought. On returning home rather late at night, I slowly crept upstairs and went straight to bed. All through the night, I could not sleep. I was tossing and turning every few minutes and my feet were still cold from the return journey. As I lay on this bed trying to get some sleep, my mind was in complete turmoil. My mind was disturbed by what the preacher had said and I knew that God was challenging me to give my life to him. My mind would not rest from the earlier text and God was asking me to follow him. He had died for me so that I can have full forgiveness of my many sins. The words written on the blue cloth on the pulpit kept on flashing in my mind every few minutes. I was very reluctant to "Follow Him". I was very reluctant to give my life to the Lord but the call continued to persist with agony, I could not get any rest until I surrendered my life to Christ and decided to follow him. This decision was not an easy one but the right one. This decision has had an everlasting effect on my life and throughout my life, God has been faithful. Through this decision, I have assurance, forgiveness, and peace with God. Not the sort of peace which the world gives which will last only for a short time, but God's peace will last for eternity.

Over the years, numerous people have asked why I changed from Sikhism to Christianity. Yes, indeed, why did I change? I believe there is a vast difference between Sikhism and Christianity. There is a vast difference between Christianity and all other religions. With Sikhism, it is a way of living but with Christianity, I do not have to rely upon good works as do all the other religions because forgiveness and mercy have already been attained by Christ on the cross. I no longer have to rely upon my good works because I have none. This was a complete transformation for my life. I am writing this at the age of 72 years and I can say with full confidence that this was the right decision for me to make. Since the age of 15 years, I have been a follower of Christ without any regrets. This does not mean that my life has been easy. I have endured the same trials and tribulations as other people have experienced, but God has been standing by my side to support and comfort me. Hence, I have no regrets but only confidence that one day I shall be with him in eternity. What else can I ask for? As far as I am concerned my future is secured by the one who died for me and gave himself for me. I can stand before God, not trusting in my good works but trusting in the sacrifice made by Christ on the cross on my behalf.

Chapter 11

Life at Home in the 1960s

After a couple of years being in England, as a family, we began to settle down into our new surroundings and the new customs at home, school, and the church. Our written and spoken language began to improve and I started to have more confidence in what I was doing and perhaps embarked on making my own decisions and becoming more independent. This growth was natural. Subsequently, living at home with my parents, life was becoming quite uncomfortable and at times quite difficult. As time went on, I would call it unbearable. As I mentioned earlier, I did not know Dad that well. He was not around during my early years and he was not around a great deal when we were living together in Wolverhampton. Work was his life and he worked extremely hard to support us. He took supporting the family very seriously. Due to his illiteracy, he could only find manual work which was hard work and very demanding in the early sixties and Dad was employed as a labourer in the foundry and then later on as a Slinger at Wednesbury Tube Company, which was on the other side of Bilston. This was hard and thirsty work and also the wages were very low as a labourer, so he worked as many hours as he could to support us. The normal working week at that time was 45 hours per week which was later reduced to 40 hours per week for manual workers only. White-collar workers at the time enjoyed a shorter working week and many other privileges. There was a lot of disparity between the manual workers and the office workers at that time. However, quite often Dad would work about one hour overtime every day, and then he would work half a day most Saturdays and on occasions a half-day on Sundays which was at double time. This meant that he would work half a day for a full day's wage. He would come home exhausted and the week would be never-ending. On weekdays, he would come home about 7 pm, have his meal and go to bed around 8 pm and then he would get up just after 6 am. Having had his meal, either Satvant or I would have to fill a bowl of warm water and a towel and bring it into the lounge and put it on the carpet in front of him whilst he sat on his green plastic chair. It was our duty every day to wash his feet and dry them with a towel and then discard the dirty water. He expected that to be done without any question. His view was that he worked long hours to support the family and therefore, he should be treated as such. Children were treated as subservient. This type of lifestyle carried on for years. He worked very hard to sustain the family income. So you can understand why the rest of the family did not see him much nor had a strong relationship with him. Whilst all this was going on, we as children were changing, growing up, maturing, becoming educated, becoming aware of the English culture, and becoming more independent and confident. Although all this was taking place, Dad was very much living in his Indian dream world and expecting all of us to be obedient Indian children in every way. There was no discussion on any subject and there was very little communication within our family. What he said went. It had to be done, whilst at the same time, I was becoming more independent and trying to make my own decisions as teenagers did and still do. At the weekend, if he was not working, he would go down to the market in Wolverhampton and he would do some meat shopping. Wolverhampton had an inside market as well as an outdoor market. The outside market consisted of stalls selling vegetables, fruit, household goods, and so on, whereas the inside market stalls sold meat and fish. As you walked along the aisles you would see rows of chickens, rabbits, and a few ducks still with their feathers hanging along the top railings. We would walk from one aisle to the next looking for bargains. He would usually buy a feathered chicken which had to be plucked, deskinned, and then chopped into small pieces for the Saturday night curry. Almost on every occasion, he would call at the pub on the corner of Great Brickkiln Street, Wolverhampton for a pint or two. This pub is near to where the Sainsbury store is now located. I know this because, on the odd occasion, I accompanied him to the market, I had to stand outside and wait for him, whilst he had his treat. I was never offered any drinks or crisps. In those days, these pubs were drinking places for adults only.

Mum on the other hand had a nice and relaxed personality. She was very easygoing in comparison to Dad, but she had no power or control or say as she was also illiterate and not earning. She was the typical Indian housewife. She knew her role within the family and carried on regardless. I don't know what went on without my knowledge but there was always some tension between the children and Dad, but part of this was the influence of the new culture. The main issue was that in our parent's eyes, we were not good Indian children especially us, the boys, in the eyes of the Asian community. We would not attend various functions within the Asian community, as these functions would mainly take place on Sundays, which for us was a church day. We would not go out to the pubs and our parents were being put under great pressure by the community, for us to conform within the Asian community and comply with their cultural expectations. It has to be understood that in the 1960s, the Asian community was quite small. The community was dependent upon each other and they knew each other. They depended upon each other for support, work, communication, and social events. They had family gatherings, men drinking together, meeting at the Gurdwara together, and weddings within the community. The Asian social network was very limited. They also depended financially on each other. They started their own saving system. In those days, if you were out of work, your friends would ask their employer if they needed another employee. This was the practice within the community. So, the community played a major role in the lives of our parents and others in a similar situation. Whilst all this was going on, my brother and I had several offers of marriage proposals over a while and each one was declined. Depending upon Dad's work situation, we would have several visitors on a Saturday night. The men would go out drinking and after they had consumed several pints, they would come to our house to further indulge in socializing. This is when the whiskies, brandies, and other spirits would come out. When they had had enough, they would feast on the meat and other curries, whilst we the children waited on them and the ladies cooked. Having consumed so much alcohol, then the arguments and the skeletons in the cupboards would come out. They treated us as outcasts because we would not conform to their lifestyle.

There was tremendous joy in the home when my two younger sisters were born. The eldest Satvinder Kaur came into the world on the 23rd. August 1961 and Jaswinder on 27th. December 1964. I said there was tremendous joy, which is true but Mum and Dad would have preferred boys rather than girls. The reason being, then they would not be responsible for the dowry or the majority of the wedding cost. The Indian custom is that the bride's family is responsible for the dowry and for hosting the wedding reception plus other exchanges of gifts.

I could say that hot bedding was first invented by the Asian Community. In the 1950s and 60s, the Asian community was very small. Dependency upon each other meant survival. They had their supporting guidelines. When a person from India, especially from their local village or district was arriving in the UK, someone from the community would fetch him from the airport. Until he found employment, he would stay rent-free in the house which would be already overcrowded. He was allowed to eat anyone's food without any questions being asked. He would just look after the house. Most of the residents worked on night shifts; therefore, there would always be an empty bed available. This is hot bedding. This could carry on for few months until they found work and only then, they would contribute towards the rent and other utilities. I visited some of these terrace houses near Chapel Ash, near St. Marks Road, Wolverhampton. Some of these houses have now been demolished.

Chapter 12

The Runaways

The offers of marriage proposals were becoming a major issue, to the extent that it was leading to major and constant bitter arguments at home between Dad and me. Satvant had already run away from home following his farcical marriage proposal to which I shall return to later. What now? Dad was miserable, grumpy, and very unhappy with the events regarding his eldest son's failed engagement. Dad was under the impression that if he could get the children married off, then all the children would be off his hands and no longer his responsibility. Being the next eldest living at home, I was now the target to get off his hands. This became a major source of arguments. I was always thinking about what was going to be his next step. He was finding it very difficult to face other people within the Asian community. His perception was that other Indian families were perfect. They had perfect sons and daughters, as they all lived at home and attended the local Gurdwara. However, were they? This was the question on my mind. I suppose it depends on from whose perspective that you are considering this from. All Asian families had their issues and difficulties which we became aware of later on. The same applies to most families. In some of the Asian families, there was a complete breakdown. We were not unique or different from other families, except that our disagreements and arguments were always blamed upon our newfound Christian faith which was unacceptable to them.

As a family, we moved house from Newhampton Road West to Bushbury Road, Heath Town, Wolverhampton, which was on the other side of the town in 1965. This was a semi-detached house and this house gave us a bit more space. It had a small garden at the rear and a wooden gate leading to the back door entrance. We had no garden furniture and Dad had piled few bricks and made two lob-sided pillars with a wooden plank and made it into a bench to sit on. He would sit there and soak up the sun on the odd occasion when he was not working. This house was situated on a busy main road but it so happened that it was within walking distance of my workplace.

One night, whilst living at Bushbury Road, one of my siblings had a huge argument with our parents and left the house very early the following day without telling anyone. When this was discovered, Mum and Dad were under the impression that they had left home. I recall Dad sitting on this lob-sided bench being aggressive, shouting at Mum and blaming her for the incident. He and I then spent most of the day looking for them hoping they would turn up. I made numerous phone calls but with no success. Mum would then start to sob and tears would roll down her cheeks, eyes full of water which she would wipe with her chuni, which was wrapped around her neck most of the time. She would avoid Dad like the plague. She would try to cook but her heart was not in it. Cooking was then a chore for her. She would not eat because she was worried about her children and she was especially worried about her missing child at the time. She was restless and at a loss over what to do, but I know that there was nothing that she could do. Dad on the other hand, never lost his appetite, even in these uncomfortable circumstances. Food was the highlight of the day for him without fail. On that warm summer day, he sat on that bench with the plastic chair being placed in front of him and food placed on it for him to consume. He didn't even get up to wash his hands after he had eaten. Then, there would be the demand for tea with sugar which had to be stirred for him. There was no communication between any of us and you could cut the atmosphere with a blunt knife. No one could be seen as having a good time or even a smirk. It was obvious that we were all worried and concerned. This was a self-generated situation and it could have been avoided with a little thought and compromise. I do have some idea what led to that situation, as I recall having to deal with it. I would try to keep out of the way but every time I left the house there was an interrogation as to where I was going, who I was seeing and when I would be returning? Dad was under the impression, that I was not telling him and that I knew where they were which I did not. They came home later on that evening which was a big relief to us as a family. Dad just would not face up to the cause of the argument. I suppose in a way that was a good thing, as it may have led to another showdown and the incident being repeated. This sibling told me several years later that they had not run away or left home but they had gone to see their friend.

As was the Indian custom, Parminder was the first one to accept an arranged marriage and she was married to a young man who came from India. His name was Satpal Singh. Following their wedding, they lived off Cannock Road in Wolverhampton. Frequently they would visit us in the evening. Their first child Samo was born there.

Another one of my siblings, who also wishes to remain anonymous, had to deal with a similar situation but a lot more serious. Although I do not recall there being any arguments about the subject of arranged marriage, Dad had arranged her marriage and even had the wedding invitations printed without her knowledge. He never consulted her or mentioned anything to her. This did result in an argument and consequently them leaving home and going into hiding so that Dad would not be able to make contact or find them. At the time of this incident, this sibling was working for a small company, which was situated on the corner of Wednesfield Road and Woden Road in Wolverhampton. This company was about 100 yards away from my workplace of Chubbs and Sons. Chubb subcontracted some of their work to this company. As they went into hiding, their arranged marriage never took place. Having left home under these awful circumstances, they never returned home. From that moment onward, Dad disowned his child. They were considered by Dad as nonexistent and if someone asked him about his children, he never included them. Both Satvant and I tried to make contact and support them in their unique situation but there was no contact from them until after few weeks at which time they were coping.

Chapter 13

The Runaway Groom

Well, where is he? I have spent hours looking for him. He must be found and found very quickly. The stress was escalating exponentially every second and every minute. The clock would not stop ticking. Would the time stop to give us some leeway or some grace? The tension was rising. You can get lost in someone else's sadness and that was exactly what was happening here. Tears running down Mum's face and no one was able to console her. She was beginning to age even within few hours of the situation being discovered. What could we do? What would happen if we can't find him? The pain was becoming unbearable. There were no easy answers. All Dad asked him to do was to come and meet him with the others. What could be wrong with that? The situation was deteriorating by the minute as the evening sun was casting its own shadow beyond the clouds as they spread their wings over the fathomless sky. The night was falling and the darkness was shrouding every corner of the house despite the lights being on. Their sorrow was so deep and it could not be compared to any situation Mum and Dad had encountered previously in their entire lives.

Satvant had yet another marriage proposal which he declined, but Dad knew better than anybody else. Dad had agreed for Satvant to marry this young Indian girl whom he had never met or agreed to marry. Despite declining the offer, engagement arrangements had been made and the invitations for the engagement ceremony had been issued. This was going to be a great celebration within the Kalu family for this forthcoming engagement followed by the wedding. I had no idea what was going on until few days before this event. This was taking place the following Sunday. All the food, including the Indian sweets, whisky, brandy, and other alcohol and music including the cultural and customary exchange of gifts had been arranged without any consultation or family discussion. The only information that I was made aware of was that I must stay at home this coming weekend. This means no church this coming Sunday or any other kind of social life. However, unknown to me or anyone else in the family Satvant had other plans. On the Thursday before the Saturday, he had completely disappeared. There was no trace of him. When all this came to light, both Mum and Dad were extremely traumatized and did not know which way to turn to or where to seek any confidential help. The atmosphere at home was very intense. It was so intense that you could stand your spoon in it. No one was speaking to each other and both Mum and Dad were constantly arguing and blaming each other and shouting at the children. If only the boys had been brought up properly, we would not have had this problem. I remember Dad getting hold of his friend Resham who was the main instigator in these arrangements. We knew him quite well and it was his family that we shared our little terraced house with when we all came from India. He was the only person with transport and he was the major player in these arrangements. Anyway, he came over with his wife to our house immediately. Mum started to cry and tears were rolling down her face and she did not know what to do or where to turn to. She felt miserable and she looked miserable. Her stomach must have been churning over. This unforeseen situation was completely out of the blue and beyond anyone's control. No one was in control of anything. It was completely out of their depth. What could she do anyway? She probably had no say in the situation. Just to cope with or avoid the situation, she started to cook, and then she would just come and sit down and get up again. Tears were streaming down her face and she was completely inconsolable. Cooking food that no one wanted to eat. It was quite a unique situation to deal with. In the meantime, I was getting the brunt of the blame. In the midst of it all, Resham came up with a plan.

I was at home trying to keep out of the way, neither to be seen nor heard and wishing that I could also disappear into a vapour. However, that was impossible as I daren't go out, as that would be the case for yet another argument and blame but on this occasion, I would be in contempt. Contempt of Mum and Dad's way of life, a direct defiance of their culture, their values and outright disobedient. Complete contempt of arranged marriages. The consequences of the aftermath just would not be worth it, so, I decided to sit it out and face the consequences. When Mum or Dad would walk in, my eyes would be fixed on the Television as if they were not there. This was the only way out. There was nothing that I could have done. I felt hemmed in and out of control. According to my parents, the church was the culprit in splitting up the family. If only the boys went to the Gurdwara and mixed with other Indian families and went to the pubs and so on, then that would be alright and acceptable. We would not be behaving like this and bringing disgrace and shame on our family. So, what was the solution? How were they going to deal with this? I was under immense pressure just being at home. I wished I wasn't there. Being male, able to speak the language and being familiar with Satvant's friends from the church, and also knowing where his friends lived, Dad and Resham concocted their plan. They demanded that I take them to the homes of our friends at the church to look for him. They had no option but to find him. I had no choice except Hobson's choice. I wasn't asked but just told again and again that the church was to blame for creating this awful unbearable situation and destroying our family. There was no recognition that they should take some responsibility for this situation and their actions.

Following Resham and his wife's arrival, I reluctantly walked towards his car and got into the car which was parked just outside the house blocking some of the traffic. Having got into the car, I even more reluctantly directed the car to Jim's house. All the way, I was getting hot, sweaty and distressed. Numerous questions were going through my mind but with no answers. Secretly praying, but praying for what? What will happen if he is there? What are Resham and Dad going to do when they see him? Will he make a run for it? Will they force him into the car and asking for me to assist them? Does he not see the turmoil that he is causing the family? All these thoughts were going through my mind. I was becoming even more restless. We reached Jim and Eileen G's house and they sent me to knock on the door and ask if Satvant was there, or whether they knew where he could be as we needed to find him urgently. I reluctantly knocked on the door, shaking and hoping he would not be there. I knew the consequences. The door was answered by Jim who looked surprised to see me standing at the door. Perhaps he was half expecting someone to turn up looking for Satwant. It would be very unusual for me just to turn up at their house. So I asked Jim the question and it appeared that he did not know as to where the culprit could be. Having done this, my next visit was to the home of John and Sylvia W, who lived on Uplands Road, Bradmore. Again the feeling of stress and the emotional drain were even more intense and so was the response. These were the only two homes visited that evening as it was getting a bit late. It transpired later that they did not know as to Satvant's whereabouts either. Both John and Jim knew that Satvant was going to go into hiding but had no idea where. These arrangements had been previously and mutually agreed upon so that they could reply honestly to my questions.

What would be the next biggest question? How could this situation be resolved without Mum and Dad losing their face in the family and the community and the Gurdwara? What are they going to say to the bride's family? How are they going to take this bad news? What exactly is the family going to do? Remember, the engagement invitations had already gone out and we now have further complications. What are they going to do? Well, the show must go on regardless of the circumstances. Following discussion between the families and definitely without any consultation and unbeknown to me, they had agreed that I must be the substitute groom. I must take up Satvant's place and be engaged to this girl. So, I was to be the second choice to take his place. How could this be? Was it a football match that I could be a substitute for? There had been no discussion or any form of consultation with myself. They told me that I have no choice but to get engaged to this young lady whom I had never seen or had any intention of seeing. I just was not prepared for this sudden enforced engagement. I had no chance to escape but I was caught in the fisherman's net. No breathing space. No choice. There was no fifty-fifty, or phone a friend. I was there as the sacrificial lamb. It was my job and my duty to save the family's face or face their wrath. They were all watching me like a hawk, in case I tried to fly the net.

On Sunday morning as part of the engagement ceremony, I had to take an early morning bath and then had to get dressed in my smart clothes. This was followed by the incense being burned and swung around Guru Nanak's poster and prayers being said to him. As breakfast followed, the time was getting on and soon the engagement guests would be arriving.

I thought it was going to be! was I dreaming! What is going on? So where is Satvant? Is this not him? I am confused. I heard some of these comments in the background by the guests as they arrived but no one would ask openly as to what was going on. The family would neither deny nor confirm these remarks. There was a lot of tension in the background but overtly there was music being played, gallons of chai being consumed, general greetings between the families, congratulations being exchanged, empty laughter, and of course giggles and smirks behind our family's back. I did not know how to respond. Should I confirm or deny the comments? I decided that it was not my problem and therefore they would just have to deal with it. I would leave the sitting room from time to time to avoid embarrassment and not be sociable. There was always someone around me just in case I escaped.

The time had come for the execution of the ceremony "The engagement". I had to take my honourable position on a chair that was strategically positioned in the middle of the front room so that guests could go around it. Whilst sitting on the chair, I had a piece of bright coloured cloth draped from my back, over my shoulder, and resting over my lap. That cloth was draped for a particular reason. As I sat, the middleman and the two families all stood next to each other and before you knew it, they were all shaking hands, hugging each other laughing and joking. To them, it was as if I didn't exist. Despite that, the only other person missing was the young lady to whom I was getting engaged. There was no sign of her as was the custom. Maybe she had also escaped or even eloped. This was very unlikely. However, soon the presents were being exchanged between the two families. The families, including the middleman, had to present a united response to ensure that all things were going as planned. By now there was laughter and music. The next thing I knew was that Mum was entering the room again with a silver tray in her hand on which were placed quite a several different coloured Indian sweets including a couple of coconut shells and some coloured strings which were to be made into a bracelet for me. She bent down and took a ladu and broke a small portion of it. She circled this small portion over my head two to three times and then placed it on my lips. Having done that, she then took a few one-pound notes and again circled this above my head and then placed it on the cloth which was draped on my lap. She then took the coloured strings and made that into a bracelet and placed it on my wrist. When this has been done, then the bride's family did similar actions but this time it included a shirt and some money. Now it was the guest's turn to do likewise. They all came one by one; including the women, all adorned in their Sunday best and covered in bangles and bindis. They brought shirts, circled their pound notes, and placed them over the draped cloth. I had to sit there like a fool and not say anything. I was supposed to look happy and excited or even elated, but why? It had nothing to do with me. I DID NOT EVEN KNOW HER NAME! Once this has been done, it was time to celebrate, so out came more tea, Indian sweets, beer, whisky, the lot. The women in the back room sent the men in the lounge. There was then lots of singing and dancing. At least someone was happy but it certainly was not me. The guests then departed, family by family. They all said their farewell shaking hands and promising to visit each other again soon. They were looking for Satvant but what went on in our absence we do not know, we can only guess. As far as my parents were concerned it all went well. The embarrassment covered up knowing that it would soon evaporate and they would soon be back to some sort of normality. Now that the thresh hold of the day has been met, what next? After everyone had left, Dad sat in the front lounge and started to count the money that had been given as part of the engagement ceremony celebration. It was over £50 and over twenty shirts together with other presents. All those shirts were collected and taken upstairs to be stored for other people's engagements or wedding events or other family events. I asked Dad for a couple of shirts having endured the trauma of the day and he refused. I sat in the back room watching TV with whoever was at home at that time but none of my parents made any comments on the events of the day. They had nothing to say to me. They were just glad that the day had ended well despite the Run Away Groom. The fallacy of the arranged marriage now took on a different meaning.

Chapter 14

Breaking Ties

I was hopeful that peace would reign now at last, or so I thought. Maybe our relationship at home would improve. I had objectionably complied with my parent's demands. I had done everything that they had asked to ensure that all went well. What else could they ask for? I had saved the day. Now there were no more arguments about getting engaged but now there were arguments about the date of the wedding. When would I get married? The bride's family wanted to set the date. This nag kept on coming every few weeks followed by arguments and I was avoiding Dad as much as I could, bearing in mind that he was not at home a great deal. Following, yet another argument about setting the date of the wedding, I decided to leave home and go and live somewhere else. This was quite a bleak period in my life to cope with, as I was also under pressure to complete my studies as well as start my new job in a different department as a Design Engineer.

It should come as no surprise to say that I was not happy at home in my mid to late teens. I was only there because if I left, it would only cause more problems to the family. There would be more questions asked by the extended family and the community and I was not sure if I could cope living independently. Living at home had its advantages. I did not have to do any cooking, cleaning, washing up, or any other household tasks. I had no training to do these things. Would I manage to live independently or not? I was also coming towards the end of my apprenticeship in Engineering at Chubb and Sons. The wages were not great but manageable. I started to look at other opportunities such as working as an Engineer with a shipping line such as British India, (BI). They were advertising for engineers. This would enable me to leave home as this would be work-related. I started to consider the army but didn't have the guts to follow it through. This was not the sort of life that I was looking for whereas working for a shipping company would mean I had a reason to leave and be away from the pressure of the wedding pursuit. A school friend of mine wanted to travel to Spain and was looking for someone to travel with. He offered to pay in full all my costs as long as I accompanied him on his travels. I knew this was not the answer although it would get me out of the house.

With constant constraints and arguments, life was becoming intolerable at home. Maybe it was I who was the problem. Maybe it was I who was making life miserable for my parents. I am expected to love and respect my parents. Where was my obedience? These questions kept on coming to mind and on occasion, I would question myself. Self-examination is a good thing. Then, my mind would go to my colleagues at work or the people at our church who have always been supportive of me. I could understand if I was being difficult but the wedding saga and the church issues kept on being resurrected again and again. In the end, I decided it was time to act. It was time to take action. It was time to fight back. It was time to stand on my own two feet. It was time to be independent whatever the cost. You cannot escape the reality of life. Life was to be explored. So, the decision had been made whatever the cost. It cannot all be negative, there must be some advantages. Get up and go and have some confidence in yourself. There must be other people in worse circumstances than me.

From that day onward, I would frequently buy the Express and Star and troll the local newspaper in the "Rooms to Let" for bedsit accommodation and look for a bedsitter to rent. The bedsit would only be one room with a bed, a small portable cooker and a sink in the same room with some access to a shared bathroom. I knew what the accommodation would be like as I had a friend at the church who was living in a bedsit. I spoke to him few times and also had visited his bedsit. I was not going into a situation with closed eyes. It was not easy to get rented accommodation if you were from the immigrant community due to racial discrimination. Some even put up notices in their windows saying "No Blacks" to discourage the immigrant community from even applying for rented bedsits. The immigrants were classed as second-class citizens. They were not treated as equals. If you were white then that was no problem. I looked at few bedsits; being Asian they would either put the rent up substantially or would say that the accommodation has been taken and was no longer available. Asian and Afro Caribbean people were not welcomed at most places, especially when it came to offering or letting accommodation. After much searching, I eventually found a place just off Lea Road in Wolverhampton and I was hoping to move in there in a couple of weeks once the current occupier had left. I had agreed to take on the bedsit but was not looking forward to it. However, needs must and maybe I could find something a bit better later on. That was my thinking. One of our church attendees was a young man by the name of David D, who was not an immigrant but he was living in a bedsit and he was just about managing. He did not seem to have any worries. He invited me to come and look at his bedsit which I did. It was just about adequate but very limited. At home, I had all the physical comforts and even luxury compared to this bedsit but inside I knew I had to take the final plunge. Sometimes mental and emotional needs override the physical ones. The decision had been made. It so happened that I was talking about leaving home to a friend at church and he or she passed this information on to the Minister of the church that I attended. The Minister then, unknown to me, had a word with a family within the church and this family offered me temporary accommodation. I moved in with them on March 11th, 1972. Their names were Chris and Alan B and they had a very young daughter, Carole Anne. They accepted me fully as I was and with no conditions attached. They showed love and respect, regardless of the baggage that I was carrying. They were a lovely family and they were pillars of support to me especially as when I left home I was at a very low ebb. They lived at The Nurseries in Coven. This was convenient in some way as I was not living near my parental home. I have the greatest respect and admiration for both Chris and Alan and almost 50 years later we still have contact with each other from time to time. They are a wonderful couple. My wife and I went to see them in 2019 and caught up with each other. Alan's health is deteriorating due to age but he is one of the kindest people that I have come across.

I had been considering leaving home for several months but plucking up the courage was a different matter. It is a bit like standing on a twenty feet high diving board, looking down and having the confidence to dive in, knowing there is no midway turning back. Would I survive if I dived? Have I the guts to do it? It was not an easy decision. It not only affects you but it affects the lives of so many other people around you. People who care about you. I no longer needed the bedsit as this was going to take place, but the question was when and how? Having some support I felt a bit easier knowing that I would not be on my own and also having a decent place to live in. The decision was made. I decided to jump and pack all my belongings without raising suspicion to anyone else in the family. I knew that if my parents found out there would be a massive argument which I wanted to avoid. There would be a lot of shouting and of being ungrateful to them. What would the community think? So why cause any more problems when you do not have to.

I considered everything carefully, weighing up the pros and cons, not that there was a great deal of choice. Satvant was now no longer living at home but I was sharing the bedroom with my younger brother Gurnam. During the week preceding my manoeuvre, I was trying to put some of my things together such as my passport, my Naturalization document, my certificates, some photographs, and other relevant papers which seemed important at the time. This also included some of my work equipment. I managed to find most things and steadily started to put some of my clothing together but not quite. As I recall, it was Saturday morning around 10-30am, I was gathering all my belongings when unexpectedly Satvinder, my younger sister came upstairs to the bedroom without knocking and she said that Mum was asking for her weekly board money. I was completely taken aback by that request as it had never happened before. I could not think of what to say and almost freaked out, so, my reply was quite blunt. Tell her that I am not going to pay board and lodgings because I am leaving home. What else could I say? Within two or three minutes of saying that, I threw everything I had in my draws into the bag haphazardly and came down the stairs and straight out of the door, throwing all my belongings into the back of the car and driving off as quickly as I could. I didn't even say goodbye. Upset and scared. I drove for a while and then took a breather. I was in shock that I had done it. Was I being stupid? No, it cannot be entirely my fault. If only they had listened to what I was saying. There was no leeway. At least I am now out of the house. The deed is done, right or wrong. It's happened. Life will never be the same again and it wasn't.

Chris and Alan were a lovely family. I got on well with Chris, Alan, and Carole Ann and it was a happy time for me as I had never experienced friendship and encouragement like that previously. They treated me well. It was the right place. There had been so much negativity in my life and they were such an encouragement. Alan worked as a driver for Goodyear Tyre Company on Stafford Road, Wolverhampton. He enjoyed listening to music and going to football. He introduced me to the voice of Mario Lanzo. Together, with others, we went to see Pele play at the Aston Villa football ground. That was a terrific night. Alan's car broke down on the way back and he was on an early shift at work the following morning. Chris on the other hand worked very hard to care for Carol-Anne and ran the children's club at Merridale Church where I also helped. Chris and Alan also introduced me to Chris's family. I was also included in their main social gatherings. They were fun times. I lived with them for approximately seven months and whilst there I decided to purchase my own house which I did, in Lanesfield, Wolverhampton for £2,250. At that time, I had managed to save £500, of which £450 was used as a deposit and the remainder was used for legal fees, carpets, beddings, etc. Chris's help in sorting household items was invaluable. The house was at 4 Beverly Crescent, Lanesfield, Wolverhampton, Staffordshire. Following this purchase with a mortgage, I did not have a great deal of spare money but life was quiet, peaceful, tranquil, and enjoyable with lots of freedom and independence. Life was never the same again.

Whilst living with Chris and Alan, life was now on track. Both of them welcomed me into their household and their family. I enjoyed my time with them and also learned a great deal from them about relationships with other people and how to value them. On the odd Sunday, they would go for a drive and would ask me to join them. In a way, it was a lonely time living in Coven which was quite an isolated village from a young person's perspective. On the other hand, I had a good job as a Design Draughtsman at Chubb and Sons following the completion of my indentured apprenticeship. I had somewhere to live, I had a car and some cash in my pocket. Things were looking up. I managed to go on holiday and had excellent friends at church. I was happy and independent and I could not have asked for anything else. Life was good. Expenditure was a bit of an issue but I was managing fairly well with very little stress. So I thought.

The biggest challenge presented to me at that time was my parent's attitude, what people thought of them in the community, and their plans to marry their children off. This time it was not my forthcoming wedding but my younger sister Baljinder's wedding arrangements. Although I had left home, I still tried to maintain a minimal amount of contact with the family but it was not easy. I remember the first time I went home after I had left home under a stormy cloud. I would say it was more than a cloud, the shear stress of it all. Just walking away from your family, your culture, and breaking away. It would be a life of instability with no resources to fall back on. My main instinct was to survive. The advice from my church Minister was to go back and see them a few days after leaving home. This was quite difficult but I felt this was the right and proper thing to do. So I decided to put this plan into action with great courage. Yes, it took a great deal of courage and letting go of self-pride and self-sufficiency. After a few days, I decided to visit the family home straight from work at the end of the day. I was very reluctant to do that. I was not at all sure how I should do that, so with great reluctance, I decided to go there straight after work, as I would have done whilst living at home without any warning. So I arrived outside the house and just sat there in my car for several minutes wondering how I should approach this. There was no way out so eventually, I took a very deep breath and decided to go. I was shaking all over and thinking whether it was all worth it? However, drawing a very deep breath, I got out of the car and entered the house through the back door as I have been doing for the past several years. Mum as usual was sitting on the settee knitting near the window, Satvinder was sitting on the opposite side and Dad was in the bathroom. Having entered the room, I said hello but there was no reaction, no response, no acknowledgment from Mum or Dad who had entered the room as I said hello. No one said "sit down" or "are you alright?" There was complete silence except for the TV blaring out. They just sat there with their eyes fixed on the Television. As soon as Dad saw me he just walked past me and went into the front room ignoring me as if I did not exist. As far as he was concerned, I was no more, I no longer existed. I just stood there gaping and wanting the ground to swallow me up that very instant. I was thinking, what should be my next move? I felt very cold, isolated, and alone and started to shiver thinking why I was bothering with this? It was very embarrassing not knowing what to do next. What should be my next move? It was so obvious to me that as far as they were concerned I was dead, especially Dad. He was not concerned about us but only about his pride in the community. I just left without uttering another word. I had done my part, or at least my duty, to make amends. It was up to them now. By now the word had spread that I had left the family home against my parent's wishes. I had brought shame and disgrace on the family and what would they say? I decided not to go and see them again as I did not want to put myself in that vulnerable situation again. It was up to them to decide the next move. I was still engaged to the young Indian lady, as far as I knew, on whom I have never set my eyes.

As I was no longer living at home and due to my constant reluctance to get married, things came to a head. The bride's family lost their patience with our family and the middle man so, they broke off the engagement. The whole episode was a great mess and could not be easily solved. As time went by, our family was asking for the jewellery and presents to be returned as it was them who broke off the engagement. My family was not taking any of the blame. Resham and a few other Dads' friends were involved in this process but only part of the gold jewellery was returned. However, that was not my problem and I was very pleased to be off the hook.

Chapter 15

Groom for Baljinder

Life was back on track again or so I thought, but you never know what is around the corner. After few weeks of sadness and disappointment, I settled into my routine of going to work during the week and church on Sundays. I was also involved in the children's work every Friday at Merridale Church. I had no regrets about leaving home. After few weeks of leaving home, I had a phone call from Dad saying that they are arranging my sister Baljinder's wedding and they needed me to come and drive them to Bradford. A telephone call from Dad was the last thing I had expected and he was asking if I would drive them to Bradford. I reluctantly agreed in the hope that maybe this would help with family relationships. From Dad's point of view, he needed a driver. As I had a car, he needed me to drive but more to the point, he needed me to go to Bradford with the others so that he could present a united front to the groom's family. He wanted to keep the family secrets, secret until at least after the event. If it had all been agreed and then there is no turning back.

It was the weekend; I left Coven where I was living at the time approximately 6-30 am to go to the family home in Heath Town, Wolverhampton for the 7 am Indian time departure. It was quite a cold and bitter morning and still dark. On arrival, there were several other people including Resham, Satpal, and Satvant. As I mentioned earlier, Resham had been instrumental in arranging Satvant's potential wedding or my engagement. We set off toward Derby to pick up the M1 and we all travelled in convoy as three or four cars were travelling together. Having just travelled a couple of miles, they all stopped for petrol for which dad paid. I had filled up the tank the night before but he never offered anything to me. The journey was very slow and uneventful except that it was very cold and the car heater was on all the way there. There were no motorways to travel on from Wolverhampton to Bradford except the M1 from Derby. We all arrived at the house and we were warmly greeted with the usual greetings. The proposed bridegroom's family lived in a two-bedroom back-to-back terrace house. There was one lounge, a very small kitchen, bedrooms, a cellar, and the toilet which was situated outside with no electric lights. Some of us sat on the chairs and the others wherever we could. The family was very hospitable. I had no idea who was who and who was going to be the bridegroom. The men had their discussion and I made no comments and neither Satvant nor I were asked about our opinion. My view was to let them get on with it. The usual fire water came out and then eventually the meal. All went well and then it was time to leave, say goodbye and return home. On the return journey, we travelled in a convoy which was fine. By now it was dark and cold and snow and sleet were coming down very heavily, so the progress towards home was even slower. The windscreen kept on steaming up and the heater was on full blast but it was still cold in the car and all the passengers travelled with their parker coats on. As I was driving on the motorway, I was in the outside lane trying to overtake another car, when for no apparent reason, my car began to lose power and also wobble a bit. So I safely returned to the middle lane and then into the first lane. By now, the car was going all over the place. We pulled up on the hard shoulder and noticed that I had a puncture and no spare wheel. As we were travelling in convoy, a couple of cars pulled up behind me, which was great. At that time there was no such thing as a mobile phone, so using the motorway emergency phone, I called for assistance. Having done that, it was agreed that only one car was needed to wait with us and two of my passengers were then transferred to other cars. The breakdown service had arrived and replaced the punctured tyre. It was then time to go and it was agreed that one of the cars would travel behind me in case there was a problem. As I set off again, for some reason there was not enough power in the engine, so I had to pull up again on the hard shoulder and again request the breakdown service. The car that had been travelling behind us as part of the convoy decided that as we have now called the breakdown service, we would be fine and another passenger was transferred from my car to their car leaving just Satvant and me. The breakdown service arrived and told us that the big ends on the engine had gone and therefore, the car had to be towed. They said they could only tow the car as far as the next service station on the motorway and no further. There was no other alternative but to accept this option. By now there was only Satvant and I left in the car as the other passengers had been transferred to other cars. We were towed to the next service station and by this time, it was around 1 am and we had just about sufficient money between us to make a telephone call to Resham and to have a cup of tea. In those days hardly anybody carried credit or debit cards and all the transactions were in cash. We were both cold and exhausted. I could not have the heating in the car on as we were being towed to the service station. Having called for help from Resham, he assured us that help is on the way. Having waited a long time at the services, Resham's son, Tarsam came with a tow rope to tow us back to Wolverhampton. We met him at the service station. His car was facing north and our's was facing south. Anyway, we got in his car and drove past the services. There were no crash barriers on the central reservation on the motorway at that time, Tarsam did an illegal U-turn on the motorway and soon hitched our car to his and we were on our way home. As we were being towed, we had to stop several times as the towing rope kept on breaking. It was bitterly cold with no heating in the car. After a long, cold and tedious journey we arrived at the family home on Bushbury Road, about 4-30 am. Dad came out to see us. Knowing that we had arrived, without even saying anything he walked back into the house. He did not even bother to ask anything. You could tell by his eyes and the expression on his face that it was entirely my fault and that we both were an embarrassment to him. Satvant was just going inside the house but as I was not asked to come into the house by Dad, I started to walk to coven. Satvant asked me to come into the house but I said to him that if Dad asked me to come inside the house then I would come in but not otherwise, as he had completely ignored me on the last occasion. Dad never came and never asked, so I had no option but to walk home from Bushbury Road, Wolverhampton to Coven which is about 6 miles away. I remember walking as the weather was so cold, frosty, and bitter. I was shivering as I walked because I was already cold from the journey having been towed with no heating in the car for about two hours. My feet were just like blocks of ice. I had not taken a big warm coat on the journey as I was not expecting to walk home. I soon warmed up as I walked. Walking through the Bushbury area is not ideal late at night or in the early hours of the morning. I had driven through this area numerous times so I was familiar with it. Every time you saw someone walking toward you, you had to be prepared to defend yourself. As I walked, I saw several people walking the streets. I eventually arrived in Coven around 6-30am, cold, hungry, and very, very tired and I decided that I will never do that again due to Dad's attitude. The least he could have done was to ask me in. It would only have been for about three hours and a cup of tea. People do not understand these situations unless they have been through them themselves. Life has to carry on regardless of the circumstances and situations especially if you have no support or very little other support. These comments are mentioned not that I am asking for pity or sympathy or to embarrass any member of the family but to explain the situation, the relationship, and the circumstances that existed between us.

There are many other experiences I could share growing up in my teens and early twenties. However, I feel that this is a good position on which to end Part 1 and you will see how my life begins to take on a different meaning in Part 2 of my life story.

Part 2

Chapter 16

New Beginning - New Life - New Family

In the early seventies, my whole life continued to evolve around Merridale Church in Retreat Street, Wolverhampton. Together, with other young people of our age, we had our Sunday Services, our social gatherings and outings. We met as often as we could and all of us were well supported by mature adults. We were invited into their homes. There was little contact between my parents and me, including other members of the family during that time and my time was occupied with church activities. Family contact also meant hassle and stress and commitment with very little benefit, not that I was only interested in the benefits. Why put up with all the hassle when there is no need, I thought. I was managing quite well and enjoying the freedom I had. We did things together with our friends from our Church, including some of the students from the Wolverhampton Polytechnic, which now has the status of a University. Life was going smoothly. I was not sure if I was going to stay single for the rest of my life. At that time, I was not aware of any Asian Christian ladies as I had broken all ties with the Asian community. Also, in those days, there were very few Asian Christian men and even fewer ladies. Therefore, any hope of meeting a single young Asian Christian lady was nil. Regardless of that, life was going to carry on and life was enjoyable.

In 1970, with other people from our Church, we went on a Christian Holiday to Oberammergau to watch the Passion Play, re-enactment of the life of Christ. This was a great and life challenging experience for all of us. There were also other people in our group. I became good friends with them, especially one young couple from London. At the end of the holiday, we exchanged addresses and they wanted me to come and visit them in London. After several weeks, following my return from Oberammergau, I made arrangements to go and visit them in London, and little did I know that they had their own agenda for my visit. They met me at London Euston station and together we went to their apartment which was located in a multi-storey building. I was so overwhelmed with their prosperity, as they seemed to have everything. The apartment looked very posh and on arrival, we had a meal. I was not used to their standard of living. On this Friday evening, they introduced me to this young Asian lady and her brother, who attended their church. There was little that I could do but socialise with her for the entire evening with other people watching us. I am not sure if she knew what had been planned for her either. I was not that happy that this had been pre-planned by this couple. What were their expectations? This was my first and last visit to them but they meant well. I never saw her again or made any effort to contact her, although she was a very attractive and kind young woman.

In September 1972, whilst attending Merridale Church, a couple of young Christian ladies, who were teachers, came to the evening service. I, together with others, had the opportunity to say hi to them later. It transpired that they had just moved into a small flat on Lea Road, which was not far away from Merridale Church. It was within a short distance of the church and I later discovered that they were newly qualified teachers and this was their first teaching post. They had both studied for their teaching qualifications at Hereford Teacher Training College. Both of them became regular attendees at Merridale Church on Sundays for the morning and evening services, as well as the midweek meetings. After the evening service on Sundays, we, the young people, would all go and visit one of the church family homes as a group for coffee, singing, and a chat. They also became involved in the youth work. This was great fun and often we laughed and joked together and we became great friends. After several months, I went out with one of these young ladies whose name was Brenda Talbott. By this time, we had known each other for several months. Her family lived in Shrewsbury. She was the eldest of three sisters. One of her younger sisters was training to be a State Enrolled Nurse in Birmingham.

By now, I was living in my own house and well settled. Francis, a newly qualified teacher, who also studied for his teaching qualification at Hereford Teacher Training College, was looking for accommodation and after a while, he moved in with me as a lodger. Brenda and her flatmate Helen and Francis knew each other through their teacher training and the Christian Union at College. I needed this additional income to help with the mortgage as my finances were very tight having to pay the newly acquired house bills. Having my own house also meant that I could invite friends around especially on Sundays. On this particular Sunday, Brenda, my lodger Francis and another friend, Bill from Birmingham were around for dinner and tea. Out of the blue, I had a phone call from Dad saying that he wanted to come and see me and that they were coming over shortly. They were coming over. Did I hear this right? It was not a question; it was a statement that they were coming over. Did I have a choice? I did not have time to think, so I had no choice but to agree. I can't move house. What am I going to do? What is on their agenda? Are they coming with yet another marriage proposal? I have visitors. Brenda is here and what shall I do with the others? Soon there was a knock on the door. DING DONG. What shall I do? Shall I just ignore them? Lots of thoughts were going around in my head but I could reach no-decision. Dad did not bother inviting me in when he should have done. Shall I treat them the same? Too late. They are here. I slowly meandered toward the door giving myself time to think and to control my thoughts. How am I going to greet them? Our last encounter with each other was met with hostilities by them. Following the last encounter, I decided not to be hurt again by their behaviour and attitude. Before their arrival, the second question was, what should I do with Brenda and the others whilst they are here? Francis and Bill are living here but Brenda... In the end, before their arrival, they all decided to go upstairs out of the way and keep very quiet. The greetings from both sides were cold and very formal. Why should they be interested in me? It's only because they want something that they have bothered. Would they have taken the trouble to come otherwise? I think not. The reason for their coming was the forthcoming marriage of my sister Baljinder to the young man Amrik Singh in Bradford. You will recall this is the family that we went to visit in Bradford when the car broke down on the return journey. They wanted me to attend the wedding so that the Sikh community would see us as a united family putting on a united front. What were my options, considering?

Brenda and I started going out with each other at the beginning of 1973 and it was great fun. We spent a considerable amount of time together due to our various church commitments and other church activities. We were both involved in the children's work as well as attendances at other regular meetings. In 1973, and before that, people from different races and cultures did not mix much with each other or date each other. This was seen as a very strange, alien, and unacceptable practice, amongst all the different communities. Each nationality should keep within their own people and culture in terms of marriage. Also at that time, there was a lot of tension building up between English people and those of darker skin. They were called all sorts of derogatory names such as wogs, dogs, etc. People of darker skin were seen as illiterate, inferior and of low intelligence. It was difficult for them to get office jobs or professional employment. During that period, there were lots of people from Jamaica and the Caribbean. Therefore, Brenda and I going out together were breaking away from tradition, pioneering new grounds and ideas. The intolerance of different nationalities and cultures went both ways. A typical example of this would be when we were living in Wolverhampton. There is a well-known park called, West Park. It is a lovely and spacious park having lots of trees, flowers, shrubbery, two small lakes separated by a small walk bridge over the waters, a children's play area, and so on. On one side, it had boats for hire and the second was pleasant to walk around. It had lots of flower beds and lovely walks. Brenda and I would from time to time take a very pleasant short walk. The areas by the flower garden were also used by around twenty to thirty elderly Sikh men, who had nothing to do all day but had to be out of their houses. They wore all shapes and sizes of various bright colour turbans. They would sit on the grass and play cards for hours on end. This was their regular social gathering place. When walking alone, there was no problem; however, when walking hand in hand with Brenda, they would not believe their eyes that we were together. They would almost come to a stop playing their cards and as we walked past them, they would all look up and stare at us as if we were aliens. From then on we would deliberately hold hands so that they could have something to look at and talk about. Also, one of the regular occurrences used to be when we were in the centre of Wolverhampton together, frequently, we would walk past Indian people walking in the opposite direction. As we approached them they would go quiet and pretend not to notice us, but when we had gone past them, to embarrass them we would turn around and watch them staring with their eyes wide open at us.

After few months of going out together one Sunday evening, I proposed to Brenda and asked her to marry me. I also asked her to think about it before answering. She asked me to get on my knees if I was serious which I did with great difficulty, as we were both sitting in the front of a Reliant Robin, which is a three-wheeler, and there is not a great deal of space in there to do that. As I was so determined, I did and it was a joy to do so. After few weeks in May 1973, we decided to get engaged despite major opposition from both of our parents. We decided not to bother with the custom of asking Brenda's parents for her hand in marriage, as we both knew what the answer would be and therefore there was no point in doing that. We both felt that it was only right that we should inform our parents that we were getting engaged. Just before our official engagement in October, Brenda had glandular fever and therefore, she was not at all well and was signed off work by her GP for several weeks. As Brenda was so poor, we celebrated our engagement by having scrambled eggs on toast! As mutually agreed previously, I also had to go and tell my parents that I was getting engaged this coming weekend. There was little contact between myself and my parents and hardly any communication, so approaching this subject was very difficult. On this occasion,

Dad was sitting in the front room, close to the fire, head forward sitting on his favourite dining room chair, that was white with a plastic flowery green base and back. The base of the chair was so hard it was like sitting on a plank of wood but this was the only chair that he could move close to the gas fire which had never been serviced. There were two of these chairs in the front room, the second he would use as a table for his roti and sabji. Very often the gas fire would give flames across the white ceramic chamber which would normally heat up and give heat. The ceramics were covered in black soot. He would spend hours just sitting there, firstly waiting for lunch and then for his evening meal, and in between, he would have two cups of tea, one in the morning and one mid-afternoon. This would break the monotony of yet another tedious day. From time to time, he would get up and walk to the window which was about six feet away to get his exercise several times during the day. The central heating would kick into action at five in the afternoon and as soon as he would hear the noise of the central heating coming on, then the fire would go off immediately. The two could not function in unison with each other. Most of the family would spend their time sitting in the back room watching TV and Mum would spend most of her time cooking, cleaning, and knitting. Doing these tasks was their daily routine. On this occasion, I too was sitting in the backroom watching the television, but on this occasion, I had a mission in mind and was waiting for the right opportunity to come my way which never did. Despite the timing which would never be right, I had to go and see him in the front room where he was sitting. I plucked up enough courage and decided to get on with it. There was an atmosphere between us as we were alone. I was nervous and wondered how to approach this subject. When I eventually plucked up enough courage, I told Dad what my intentions were but there was no response from him at all. The atmosphere in the room was cold and there was no eye contact between us. As there was no response and there was nothing else to say, I left to save further embarrassment for both of us. Was I relieved to leave the room? What do you think? I immediately left the room saying a short goodbye to the others in the dining room and made my way to the car and drove off. Grateful it had all been done. I made my way home and then, later on, met up with Brenda and told her that the mission had been accomplished as promised. She already knew what the response would be. I was completely independent and I did not need anyone's consent to get married, especially as I was twenty five years of age at that time.

Chapter 17

Our Wedding Arrangements

Life at that time was tough as Brenda and I were not supported in our decision to marry each other by either of our families. It was worse than that, as I discovered later on that several people within the church also had great reservations and they were not fully supportive of our decision. They believed that our marriage would never work out and would never last. This situation was not only alien to them but also totally unacceptable. They were nice mature people. I had known some of them for over ten years. They did not mean any harm to us but they were concerned for our welfare and our future together. Despite that, these comments were never made directly to us but I was informed of them following our wedding by a very dear friend whom we both respected greatly. This friend is no longer with us as he died following a road accident abroad.

Following our engagement in October 1973, we decided to get married on 17th August 1974 despite our family's opposition and concerns by our friends. As Brenda's parents refused to come to the wedding there was no need for us to get married in Shrewsbury, where Brenda's parents were living. This would only cause further embarrassment to them and ourselves. It was customary in those days for the wedding to take place in the bride's hometown. Given our parent's attitude, we decided that we would get married at Merridale Church in Wolverhampton. We would have the reception there too. Chris B, the family I went to live with when I left home, offered to do the catering for our wedding. This was a great relief as finances were very tight. We set the wedding date of 17th August 1974, to ensure that our closest friends were able to come as the date of our wedding was in the holiday season. Both Ministers, who were going to take part in the wedding ceremony, and Chris B and her family, who offered to do the catering were available. Once this had been sorted out, we could start thinking about getting the wedding invitations printed. We chose the face cover of the wedding invitations and then had the inserts printed separately. Twelve weeks or thereabout we started to send out the wedding invitations with RSVP and soon afterward began to get the replies back. By then, we had already booked to go on our honeymoon to Port Isaac, Cornwall. Ten weeks before the wedding taking place, there was a breakthrough from Brenda's parents, who said that they would come to the wedding and would support us. However, this set date is not convenient for them. They were going to be on holiday on that date and asked us if we could bring the wedding date forward by two weeks. If we agreed to do as they asked, then it would mean that all the wedding arrangements would have to be rearranged in less than eight weeks and also some of our closest friends would not be able to come to the wedding. However, in comparison, this was a small price to pay and all of us knew that this then would be a tremendous day for Brenda and her family. We both agreed to their request almost instantaneously.

Now that the wedding has been brought forward by two weeks, we had nowhere for the reception, no Ministers, no venue, and no church and not the company of our close friends. All our close friends were very sympathetic to our new circumstances and rallied around to support us. Having made few phone calls, we booked Harlescott Grange Evangelical Church in Shrewsbury for the wedding ceremony, which was the church Brenda attended as a youngster and the Minister of this church John B. By doing this, we knew that at least we could get married. The next hurdle was to find a venue for the wedding reception. This caused a great dilemma as most of the other nearby places were booked or too expensive until we came across Abbey Hotel, near Abbey Foregate in Shrewsbury. Although the hotel was available on the 3rd August 1974 they could not accommodate more than fifty guests but we wanted at least sixty. The time was running out as we were looking for a place in Shrewsbury but we were both living and working in Wolverhampton. It was quite difficult, but not impossible to get this sorted out. It was such a relief when both the church and the reception venue at Abbey Hotel, Shrewsbury were confirmed.

Now that the Church and the reception venue had been confirmed, both Brenda and I had to get the inserts of our wedding invitations reprinted with the new date and the venue. One of our church officers named Jim G helped us to get that sorted. In those days everything had to be hand typed on the old fashioned typewriter. It was typed on a stencil, a special thin paper with a backing, which the typewriter keys pierced. This was then layered onto the Gestetner printing machine to print manually. We had to remove the previous inserts very carefully and then reinsert the new ones with the revised information. It was quite a tricky job. The other difficulty we experienced was the compactness of the reception venue as previously mentioned. To avoid any embarrassment, we were only sending out few invitations at a time and in priority order. As the invitations were declined, we would send out the next few and hoped no one had noticed. In the end, we only had fifty two guests at the reception and even with that number, it was very crowded. The venue had a lovely garden which could be used after the reception for more photographs and socialising.

Rev. Gareth C was now no longer available to take part in the ceremony but through God's goodness, Rev John B was still available. We quickly had to reorganise the wedding ceremony or should I say rehash our plans at the last moment. We had to find an organist who would be able to play our chosen music and hymns and be available on the day. We kept the same florist. All these difficulties were sorted out with help from our friends from both of the churches. As Brenda was making her own wedding dress, she had even less time to finish this, as we were both involved in sorting out the new arrangements. Whilst all this was going on, the wedding day was approaching quickly.

The week before the wedding, Brenda went home to spend some time with her parents and the day before the wedding, Satvant, who was going to be the best man, Margaret J and I went to Shrewsbury to see Brenda and her family. It was a lovely sunny day and all of us had a good time with Brenda's family and we were all looking forward to the following day.

The day of the wedding arrived and I was feeling very excited and at the same time very apprehensive. Solemn thoughts. A lifetime of commitment. What were my parents thinking? Am I that rebellious? What if her parents have persuaded her not to turn up. Embarrassment? Pride? Rejection by my own family as well as rejection by Brenda and her family. What a thought and what a situation to contend with. There is no turning back. On the other hand, my thoughts were filled with excitement. This would be the start of a new chapter in my life. We will work things out no matter what. We do have support from our church friends. That should be enough. I think Brenda's family would help once we were married, or would they? Lots and lots of thoughts went through my mind. Now that the day of the wedding was here, several things still had to be done on the day such as picking up the flowers from the florist and then travelling to Shrewsbury to Brenda's family's house. I had to be at Brenda's house by 11 am at the latest. Travelling to Shrewsbury from Wolverhampton was a nightmare. Satvant and Margaret travelled in one car and I was driving the other in front. We gave ourselves plenty of time so that we could be there at least an hour before the start of the ceremony. We started well until we reached the outskirts of Wellington, Shropshire, travelling on the A5. This is before the days of the M54 and the other bypasses around in this area. There was a massive traffic jam due to road works and holiday traffic and the timing to get to Shrewsbury was becoming extremely tight. We were calling at Brenda's family's home first to deliver the buttonholes etc. We made our way through the traffic jam and then eventually got through it and then realised we were not going to make it on time. We pulled over and altered our plans and decided to send Margaret ahead with the buttonholes to Brenda's family and for Satvant and me to go straight to the church. This was the only way forward to save a bit of time. Margaret J had only been to the house once, which was the previous day. She was very concerned about getting lost. However, she managed.

The wedding ceremony would have been on time, except that Brenda wanted to make sure that she was late! The wedding itself was a great experience. It was a beautiful warm sunny day. The sun shone brightly and Brenda looked so beautiful in her white handmade dress, together with her bridesmaids. Rev. John B made us so relaxed at the wedding ceremony. Everything went extremely well. The service, the music, the hymns, and the ceremony went so smoothly. The wedding took place as arranged and the reception was great. It all worked out well on the day. At the reception, Brenda's Dad gave a speech then the best man and I thanked everyone for coming. It was such a wonderful occasion, which we will not forget for the rest of our lives. Following the reception, we travelled to Brenda's parent's house in Copthorne for a cup of tea and then left for our honeymoon in Worcester at the Talbot Hotel. Our original plan was to go to Port Isaac for our honeymoon but we had to make alternative arrangements and hence ended up in Worcester. The following day being Sunday, we went to church and turned up to see our friends who were at the wedding the day before. It was lovely to see them. Since the wedding, there has been harmony between Brenda's family and ourselves and they have been very supportive toward us. Over the years, we enjoyed numerous holidays together, camping and caravanning as well as going to France and Spain.

Now that we were married, what was my parent's reaction to our marriage? It was not good and there were no immediate solutions or resolutions. We were not welcomed together at their house by my parents but at the time we had sporadic contact with my sister Parminder and her husband Satpal Singh. I remember taking Parminder to Heathrow to fetch her husband from London Heathrow airport following his visit to India. We set off quite early, it was wet and cold and when we arrived at the airport, we discovered that the flight had been delayed by about three hours. We left the airport for about three hours and returned to the airport. On returning home from the airport, Parminder had prepared a meal the previous evening for us to have the next night which we all enjoyed. Around this time, I had been deprived of Indian hot and spicy food and it was a delight to eat it. It tasted incredible! She was a great cook and still is. However, from then on our relationship with Parminder and Satpal was beginning to flourish and we had regular contact with them from then on.

The relationship between us and my parents was adhoc. I would try to visit the family home alone approximately once a week. The relationship improved a little over time when Dad was not in the room but when he was there, there was always tension and atmosphere. We never visited together, as Brenda was not welcomed by my parents. As far as my Dad was concerned, she never existed and my parents never asked about her. They never asked how we were managing. All these concerns were out of the question. There existed a gulf between us and them. This rift never healed. Although both my parents went to the Gurdwara for a short time most Sundays, they were never at the centre of any of its activities. It was just a social gathering. They never mentioned who they met or saw or what they did. This was their routine. The rift between us and my parents continued for a very long time and there seemed to be no end to it.

The relationship between Brenda's parents and ourselves began to blossom following our wedding. We saw them regularly and often they would come to us or we would go to their house for meals. We went on several holidays together. Every year we would go to Mullion, in Cornwall for our summer holidays with them as well as our other friends. The children remember these holidays well.

One year, whilst we were near Mullion, we stopped on our way, at a summer fete that was being held at one of the churches. Whilst there, Brenda decided that I should take part in one of the competitive games. I reluctantly agreed and managed to get a good score with my one and only attempt. However, unknown to us, every year for several years a German lady would attend the same fete and she would be the winner of the coveted prize of a chicken. This was the ultimate prize. To win this coveted prize, she had several attempts to beat my score but eventually managed to equal it. At the end of the day, we had to compete against each other. There were so many friends and family members supporting me, she was unable to beat me. So, I was hailed as the champion with the chicken. We cooked this chicken in the evening and it was shared by at least sixteen people. Brenda's family and other friends have never forgotten the event of beating this German lady at this competition. I have been particularly asked to record this event in this book. So, here we are. As we went to Mullion for several years, the locals began to get to know us and we ended up taking part and even judging their competitions. On another occasion, the tractor and the trailer were well decorated with all the paraphernalia for another fete but were having difficulty turning into the field. In the end, our family and friends lifted the trailer and turned it, so that it could enter the field through the narrow gate. These were great holidays and the family remembers them well. As a result of this, our daughter Sarah and her family now go to Mullion every year for their annual holiday. Their children love it and look forward to it every year.

Chapter 18

Family Life

M arried life was great and we enjoyed each other's company as we still do. I worked for a small engineering design consultancy company that was within a walking distance of our house. I was well settled there as a Design Engineer. It was at the time of the miner's strike. Due to the nature of the work, my eyes began to cause some problems. Although settled, being a Design Engineer was not my chosen career. So, I began to look for alternative employment.

Leaving work aside, our first daughter Sarah was born on 12th October 1975 at Newcross Hospital, Wolverhampton on Sunday at 8:32 pm. It was a lovely, bright, and warmish day and the sun was shining. On the day, we went to church in the morning as we did every Sunday and returned home as usual for our Sunday lunch. After lunch, we would often go out for a walk or see friends as per our routine, and this afternoon was no exception. For some time, we had been contemplating moving house so that we could be near our church and other friends as they were the central hub of our lives. Also, the house that we were occupying at the time was in a subsidence area. So, we decided that we should move to a more suitable area which would be in line with our needs and requirements. On this particular Sunday afternoon, we were having a drive around the area to see what was available on the market. You will have to imagine that all this was before the emergence of the mobile phone, the internet, and social media. Whilst we were out, Brenda said that she was not feeling well and wanted to return home, which we did immediately. Little did we realised at the time that Brenda was in labour. On returning home, we contacted Newcross Hospital and they told us to bring her in immediately. She was soon on her way to the Newcross Hospital as arranged. Whilst all this was going on, my mind was racing and my thinking was in overdrive. We quickly arrived at the maternity ward of the hospital but there was nowhere to park. I was not allowed to stay with her as it was not the visiting time. I returned home and then later went to the evening service at the church which I left partway, to visit Brenda in hospital. Within four hours of Brenda being admitted to the Maternity ward, our first daughter Sarah Jayne was born on the evening of this day. Brenda and I had prearranged for me to be present during the birth. However, it was the hospital rules and regulations which must be obeyed at all times, which play a major part in our lives every day. At that time, fathers were not allowed to hold their babies in the hospital. However, that was not the case with us. After the birth, I was asked to wait outside the room, and as I waited one of the nurses who was a Christian young lady recognised me. I was soon allowed into the room and within minutes, I was holding Sarah in my arms. It was such a wonderful experience to hold your child in your arms. She was so beautiful, swaddled in a clean white towel. The visiting times were very strict and I soon had to leave.

Following Sarah's birth, on the way home, I went to see Mum and Dad and to tell them the news of Sarah's birth and I thought that there would be some acknowledgment that they had a granddaughter, but how wrong I was. Mum said, "never mind it's a girl but next time it'll be a boy" and that was about the end of our conversation. I was lost for words. There was nothing further to say or to do. I soon left to go home completely deflated and mentally dejected and exhausted. Is that it, I said to myself. It made no difference to us, whether it was a boy or a girl as long as they were healthy. This was the most exciting news to us as a family. We had become parents for the first time to a very beautiful little girl but it was only exciting to us and not to them. As far as they were concerned, Brenda and I were the outsiders. We did not belong to them, so why should they be excited. Not only this, this news, of course, would be an embarrassment to my parents, as this would leak out to other members of the extended family and into their wider circle of friends. As far as they were concerned, it was not good news at all and there would be severe and adverse comments from other people, friends, and family behind their back. When we shared our news with our Christian friends at the church, they were excited and pleased and very supportive and gave us several gifts. If we wanted to know anything that we were not sure of, they were the people to go to.

Soon after Sarah's birth in October 1975, we had decided, to definitely move to another house which would be more suitable for our needs as a family. We knew that from now on, it was going to be a challenging time and it certainly was. Firstly, becoming parents and secondly, our thoughts about moving house. Buying and selling a house for the first time. Would it all go smoothly? Could we afford it as we had just replaced our old banger with a slightly newer red VW Beetle? Which area would we like to live in? Could we still get to work from there? How about our church commitments? After a lot of consideration and prayers, we eventually plucked up enough courage and put our house on the market, but it would not sell due to subsidence in the area. We had to wait patiently but we were becoming impatient. However, one weekend we went to visit Brenda's family, and whilst there we went to Harlescott Grange church. This is the church where we were married. Whilst there, we were both challenged by God's word and we both felt God was telling us to move to Shrewsbury and to help with the work at the church in an unofficial capacity. The same thought went through Brenda's mind. We discussed the ins and outs of moving to Shrewsbury amongst ourselves as we travelled home. We wanted to be sure that this was the right thing to do and it was not our whim to do something. So, we decided to put it before the Lord so that we can ascertain God's will. We asked God to sell our house within a week if He wanted us to move to Shrewsbury. Sure enough, we had sold our house within the week and we moved to a beautiful modern three bedroom semi-detached house on Heath Farm, which was within walking distance of the church in July 1976. We settled quickly in our house and the church. It was such a wonderful experience to be at Harlescott Grange Church and we hold very pleasant memories of being part of that fellowship. Harlescott Grange church was on a local council estate, which was very deprived of local resources and it had numerous social challenges and it still does. Whilst living in Wolverhampton, I was able to walk to work in about twenty minutes, but Shrewsbury was at least an hour's drive away to work. Commuting was quite difficult but we felt this was the right place for us. At the time of our move, I was working for John A Smith, Design Consultants in Wolverhampton. They had a contract with GEC in Stafford, so I was able to travel to Stafford straight from Shrewsbury. Being a Design Draughtsman was not my passion and I wanted to change careers. I later retrained to become a Control Systems Engineer, after which I was employed by the Central Electricity Generating Board at Ironbridge Power Station until the beginning of January 1984. This again was not my cup of tea and I wanted a different challenge but which one?

Whilst living at Leighton Road, Heath Farm, Shrewsbury, our second daughter Emma Louise was born. What a morning! Whilst living on Leighton Road, Shrewsbury, Brenda and I made friends with a neighbour, Val and Don, whose back garden backed onto our back garden. They had two young children, a boy, and a girl. From time to time, we would jump over each other's fence to reach our houses. As we did not have a telephone or any other means of calling the midwife, it was agreed that we could use their house phone in an emergency. On the morning of Brenda going into labour, our neighbour Val, Don, and family were away on holiday. Nevertheless, they had left us their back door key for us to enter their house to call the midwife. Unfortunately, they had returned from their holiday a day early and on their return, they had locked the back door leaving the key in the keyhole and the door chain on. In no way, was I able to enter their house. As it was becoming an emergency by now, I called on our other next door neighbour's house and used their telephone. The baby was coming imminently; I had to ring the hospital twice and asked for urgent help. I also, asked for our neighbour to come and help. The midwife arrived and within minutes Emma Louise came into this world on the morning of 17th July 1978 around 6-45 am. It was such a relief for me never mind Brenda. We were so happy and excited knowing that our life would not be the same again.

As we were well settled, we decided to move to a larger house in 1981 which we did. We moved at the beginning of this year to The

Hassocks, which is off Featherbed Lane, Shrewsbury. A couple of miles away from our previous location and the distance was still walkable to our church. Whilst living there, our youngest daughter Lisa Nicola was born at 5-25pm at Shrewsbury Royal Infirmary on the 5th. June 1981. She was a delight to our hearts and we were so blessed as a family. Having three daughters made our family complete and kept us on our toes.

Almost before Lisa's first birthday, she began to walk and so it was time to go and buy her new shoes. A few days later, she began to drag her feet and walk holding on to the furniture, so she was taken to the doctor. The GP put this down to her new shoes. He could not find anything wrong with her and he said that as she was not in any pain, we should just monitor her for a week and if she deteriorates bring her back immediately. She continued to drag her feet, then the following morning she woke up early and I went to pick her up. "I might as well get up now as I need to get up for work shortly", I said to Brenda. I briefly sat Lisa on the carpet and Brenda noticed that she fell to one side. I picked her up again and she tumbled again, so I did the same thing for the third time and she did the same. Lisa was not in any pain and if she had been, we would have noticed this earlier. That morning we phoned the doctor. Lisa became paralysed from the waist down overnight. The GP said there is no need to bring her to the surgery again as he examined her yesterday, instead, he would like her admitted to the hospital immediately. Before going to the hospital, Brenda had to pick up a letter from the surgery. Lisa was admitted to Shrewsbury Royal hospital immediately and a few days later, she was diagnosed with Neuroblastoma on her spine. It was cancerous growth on the spine. Little had we realised that she had cancer at the age of thirteen months. What a shock, unbelief! Our world was turned upside down within a few days. From caring for a healthy baby to a baby with a life-changing prognosis. We felt devastated. Our faith in our God never faltered, He was our strength, comfort, and our guide. The following day, we were told to take Lisa to Birmingham Children's Hospital which we did in our car. On the way to the Children's hospital, Lisa started to cry and we could not console her. We ended up giving her some biscuits. We eventually arrived at the hospital and it was then that we discovered that she was to undergo surgery immediately. As we had given her something to eat on the way, the operation was delayed by two hours. Little did we know that all this would also involve overnight stays. The hospital staff was very kind to us and offered us a room in which we could stay. There was a Tesco store almost opposite the hospital. We went and brought a sun lounger to sleep on, some clothes and some food. We were so thankful that the operation was successful but sadly they were not able to remove the entire tumour. This tumour was in the shape of a dumbbell. This would mean Lisa undergoing surgery again within the next few days. Whilst all this was going on, they were doing further tests and we were informed that if the cancer had spread to other parts of her body, then they will not carry out any further treatment. What news and what trauma for Lisa? We will never forget what we had just been informed. These were life-changing moments and decisions.

Lisa had been admitted to the Birmingham Children's Hospital on a Tuesday and now it was Friday and we were concerned about our other two children, Sarah and Emma. So, it was decided that I should return to Shrewsbury and Brenda would stay with Lisa. I arrived at home around 2ish pm, immediately showered and had a change of clothing. I went to pick the children up from school and from Brenda's sister's house and following a cup of tea returned home. I had only been in the house about ten minutes when the telephone rang and it was Brenda at the other end of the line. She asked me to immediately return to the hospital, Lisa has measles. The way I felt on receiving this news was indescribable. What do I do with Sarah and Emma? I have only just picked them up and I have not seen them since Tuesday and today is Friday. With no choice, I had to contact Brenda's sister Melanie again to ask if she would continue to look after them for the time being. Having made these arrangements, I immediately returned to the hospital in Birmingham and the Pastor from our church in Shrewsbury was visiting us in hospital as I arrived. He prayed. Lisa is a fighter. Following her first surgery, she underwent another complicated operation, followed by Radiotherapy treatment and two years of chemotherapy. From 10% survival diagnosis to now being a young healthy woman who is now in her late thirties. We were also informed that she may not be able to have any children. She and her husband Matthew Wallis now have a four years old boy and two year old girl and another baby girl six months old at the time of this being written in April 2020. All this is a miracle to us and is beyond our expectations. That is why we believe in the power of Prayer.

Chapter 19

Life at Harlescott Grange Church, Shrewsbury 1976 - 1984

Harlescott Grange Church was located right in the middle of the housing estate, next to the few shops, including the fish and chip shop and the car park. Lots of young people would hang about in the car park, especially after school and during the evening. The church also used this car park for their services. Some of the young people had nowhere to go and no clubs to occupy their time. Being out on the streets, the car park became their social hang-out place. Often, they would shout abuse to the congregation or throw things at them. During the evening services, from time to time they would climb onto the roof of the church and jump about. They wanted to be chased or for someone to climb onto the roof to get them off. During the evening services, we would close the doors of the church to stop them from disturbing our services even further. We were happy for them to come in and join us and be in the warmth but they wanted to show off to their mates whether, in the church or out, it did not matter a great deal to them. This type of behaviour was frequent. During the summer school holidays, we would run a Holiday Bible Club. During one of these sessions, I remember as we got into our different groups for our teaching session, one of the young lads aged about seven years quietly telling me that his mother had committed suicide during the night. I was not sure if I had heard him right or was he having me on. What he had told me was true. He said that his dad had given him some money to buy chips for dinner and told him not to bother him for the rest of the day. This little lad had nowhere to go. He had to fend for himself with no other family members available. On another occasion, another lad of similar age came in with an axe hidden under his jumper. We had to take the axe away from him. This was normal life on Harlescott Grange Estate. We, as a family, were happy living on the Heath Farm estate which was close by. There was only a road between us splitting the estates. We did not deliberately choose Heath Farm, but this particular house was on sale and we liked it including its price which we were able to afford. Harlescott Grange Church continued to play a major role in our family life. Brenda and I became involved in the young people's lives. We were involved in Youth Work as well as teaching in the Sunday School. The families on the estate had to cope with serious social deprivation and poverty. There was massive unemployment and many families were on Social Security benefits with little money to spare for a holiday or Christmas celebrations. Some of the young people would come to our house and they would take Sarah, our daughter, out in her pram or pushchair. I specifically remember one of these young people, Yvonne F, who was a lovely young girl with a very pleasant and easy-going personality and who enjoyed taking Sarah out with her friends. A few years later she was involved in a car accident and she drowned in the River

Severn. It was so sad to see a young life come to a tragic end. We attended her funeral which was held at Harlescott Grange.

The congregation at the church was very helpful and kind. As newcomers, we became very involved in the church. Within a short time, I was appointed as a Deacon and then as a Church Secretary. I was involved, together with the congregation in the selection of their two Ministers, Michael V and Arthur O. It was a privilege to work with them.

One incident I must record here as a Sunday School Teacher. Every Sunday, after the morning service, we would run the Sunday School for the young people. As previously mentioned, the attitude of some of the young people was very hard and they were difficult to control. One of the rules that we insisted upon was not to use swear words. On this particular Sunday, the young people were very hyped and difficult to control. Then one of the lads who wanted to show off to others began to swear. I asked him not to use this language again but he would not. In the end, I asked him to leave the class but he refused. I insisted that either he apologise or leave. Within minutes, his mates began to say, "if he leaves, then so will I". By now there were several of them of the same mind. I still insisted that he should leave which he eventually did. Then they all followed this lad out except for one young girl. The following week, they all came back and apologised for their behaviour for the previous week and behaved. This just gives you a flavour of the type of young people on the estate that we were dealing with. However, regardless of the incidents such as these, we were able to work with some of the young people and formed a good relationship with them.

In January 1981, we moved to a larger modern new detached house just off Featherbed Lane, Harlescott. It was 1, The Hassocks. This was a lovely modern house and it was more than a comfortable house for our needs. It gave us space, new neighbours, a large garden and it was easier to commute to work from there. By moving into this accommodation, we were able to be hospitable to some members of our congregation. Work, church, and family life kept us busy but as I was working at Ironbridge Power Station on shifts, I could not face doing shifts for the next thirty years so we had to make a move. I gave a lot of thought to what else I could do nearby, but there was nothing viable. I had to do something that I enjoyed! but what? that was the question. Otherwise, life would just drag on and on and I would be stuck in a rut. Something had to give way. My thoughts of becoming a Probation Officer or a Social Worker began to resurrect again and I began to ponder if that could be a possibility. In my younger days, I worked as a voluntary Youth Worker with the young people in Wolverhampton at least two nights a week which I thoroughly enjoyed. So, I further considered the possibility of this type of work. To pursue this type of career, I had to retrain. My original intentions were to study for these professional qualifications at Wolverhampton Polytechnic, which was within a commuting distance from Shrewsbury, but I was unable to secure a place there. Therefore, I had to look at other options. I was eventually offered a place at Leicester, which is now the De Montfort University, to study Social Work, so we had very little choice but to leave Shrewsbury. As a family, we moved to 8 Lowcroft Drive, Oadby, Leicester, in May 1984. Moving away from Shrewsbury, from our fellowship, Brenda's family and our very close friends with whom we had formed very strong relationships was very sad but there was little choice. We continue to have contact with these friends after all these years. They were such a blessing and encouragement to us as a family. We frequently visit Shrewsbury, as Brenda's family are still living in that lovely part of Shropshire.

Chapter 20

My Chosen Career

Having moved to Shrewsbury in the very hot summer of 1976, commuting between Shrewsbury and Wolverhampton or Stafford was becoming difficult and burdensome. Not only that, I was not enjoying my work. The journey every morning and afternoon was becoming tedious and stressful. I never wanted to be a Design Draughtsman in the first place and it all happened by default. My eyes were experiencing a considerable amount of strain due to the detailed work that was expected. Working from nine till five with a lunch break in between was affecting my eyesight. How on earth did I end up as a Design Draughtsman? Draughting, technical drawing as it was known in school, was one of my weakest subjects. On completing my apprenticeship in 1969, I was still completing my studies in Engineering. I was in between being a blue-collar worker and a white-collar worker. I wanted to be a white-collar worker and who would not in those days? I wanted to enjoy the additional privileges offered to white-collar workers. Initially, a Detail Design Draughtsman was the only position I was offered with no other choice so I took it. This was in the middle of my studies and I was not able to leave for alternative employment with another company. I stayed with Chubb and Sons Ltd until 1973 and in between, I moved departments. Within a short time, I was offered the position of Standardisation, Rationalisation, and Metrication Engineer. This was an advisory position within the company. I enjoyed exploring the company in greater detail. Everyone in the Department was coming to me for advice on metric values and standards, even people in senior positions. I even ended up attending one of the Directors' Board Meetings to give advice. I had a lot of freedom to talk to people on the shop floor as well as with the management. As it is with most jobs, these positions do not last for long. After few months, new Management came and caused a great deal of havoc to most of the workers in the Department. Numerous people were unhappy and several people left within months and I was one of them. I soon found employment as a Design Engineer with a consultancy company. Hence the reason for the commute between Shrewsbury, Stafford, and Wolverhampton.

Having resigned as a Design Engineer, I trained to be an Instruments and Control Loop Systems Engineer in Wrexham in 1977. Having completed this training, I was offered employment at Ironbridge Power Station, where I worked from January 1978 to January 1984. During that period, I finally decided that engineering was not for me. Engineering was the job that I landed following my session with the Careers Advisor. Opportunities were very few for immigrants unless you were a blue-collar worker. There was a significant difference in the status and working conditions between a blue-collar worker and a white-collar worker. So, where do I go from here? I suppose the only status that I can recall whilst working at John A Smith was when I did some design work on the Concord air conditioning system that had now long faded into my distant memory.

Soon after our wedding in August 1974, I saw an advert in the Express and Star, the local evening newspaper in Wolverhampton about a career in the Probation Service. This was of some interest, so I called in at their head office. Having spoken to the person concerned, they advised me to secure a place at a university to study for this profession and then come and see him. According to him, I would be funded. I considered Birmingham University for this qualification and I knew that this opportunity would be life-changing and the university was within a commuting distance by train. However, within weeks we discovered that we were expecting our first child and so our plans were put on hold as mentioned previously and also we had decided to move to Shrewsbury. So, nothing became of that opportunity until 1983 when I reached the point of no return of pursuing a career in Social Work. As most of my training and qualifications were in engineering, these qualifications were not classed as academic. So, not having academic qualifications, it was very difficult to secure a place at any university. However, Nottingham Trent University became interested following my application to them but they advised me to reapply the following year as they had already taken their full quota of students for the coming year. The second option was Leicester Polytechnic who offered an interview. Following this interview, I was offered a place at Leicester and I started my training in Social Work in January 1984. For the first four months, Brenda continued to live with the children in Shrewsbury and I lived in Leicester midweek and returned to Shrewsbury at the weekend. Initially, studying at this level was more than a struggle as there was so much written work involved including several essays, seminars, dissertations, and exams in the second year. I was not used to this type of academic study. It was very, very demanding. To top it all, there was also the Social Work placement at Kettering Social Services Department and Northamptonshire Probation Service as well as analysis of the placements. With hard work, patience and perseverance, I gained my qualification in Social Work. It was now time to celebrate and start a job that I would enjoy.

It was now time to embark on my new career and start using my qualifications. I did not have to wait for long, as I started my first job with Leicestershire two days after being qualified. Since then, I have been involved in Social Work in one way or another.

To further my career, I left Leicestershire Social Services in September 1991 and took up my new position as Principal Social Worker with Northamptonshire. Being based at Briar Hill, I handled some of the most difficult child protection cases for two years, after which I thought it was time to move on which I did. My new position took me into assessing children who had an educational statement and to consider if they met the disability criteria under the 1976 Disability Act or not. This post I enjoyed with immense pleasure and I looked forward to going to work each day. It was so pleasing to be of some assistance and encouragement to the parents of the disabled children. They appreciated the support given to them, which was opposite to the attitude of people I had dealt with in Child Protection. I was in this new post for three years and as often happens, the Social Services Department was reorganised and my disability post no longer existed under their new plans. Following this reorganisation, I became a Principal Care Manager until September 1999. I left Northamptonshire and took up my new position with Warwickshire County Council, Social Services, as a Team Manager. I was enjoying this post until the new Management decided to realign the existing structure, after which the whole department went downhill. Numerous people left, low morale, budget issues, and so on. With the pressure of work, constant strain and no support from Management, I began to have health issues and eventually took early retirement at the beginning of 2003. Having left the Department, I discovered later that the majority of the middle Management resigned en block due to issues arising from realignment. Now although retired, I soon found employment with a consultancy agency which I thoroughly enjoyed.

Due to commuting, I left the agency and I was then employed as a Senior Social Worker, dealing with difficult cases. One of those cases had quite an adverse effect on my health. One of the clients held a colleague and me as a hostage at knifepoint in Melton Mowbray. There was very little chance that we would come out of this incident alive but we did. We were eventually rescued by the Police. Every workplace has its issues, pressure of work and high demands. About eighteen months after this incident, I decided to retire completely from Social Work. It was quite a potted and varied history in Social Work and during these years, I dealt with almost every type of social work case, including fostering and adoption, international adoptions, children and adult mental health, older people mental health, learning disability as well as physical disability, child protection and so on. There is very little in Social Work that I have not dealt with. I feel that I have achieved my goals in my career with little or no regrets. I felt I should have been in this career from the very beginning, after leaving school. I suppose, on the other hand, these opportunities were not available in the late sixties and very early seventies as my education would not have been sufficient to do this type of work. I would not have had the ability to study at this level in my late teens and early twenties. In the end, it all worked out fine with no regrets.

I also served as a Magistrate, "Justice of the Peace" (JP) from July 2009 for Leicestershire and Rutland until September 2017. This position gave me a greater insight into the workings of the Justice system. As a magistrate, I dealt with quite a mixture of cases ranging from a speeding fine to a murder case which was passed on to the Crown Court. As a Bench, we dealt with a rugby player, basketball player, drugs, remands, firearms and other similar related cases including a visit to the prison. As a magistrate, it allowed me to sit with various Judges at the Crown Court and listen to the appeals against the sentences imposed by the Magistrate Courts. This was quite an eye-opener. I had to retire from sitting as a Magistrate on reaching the age of 70 years. This position I really enjoyed and I looked forward to all of my sittings. I could write about several interesting cases I dealt with, but there are too many to mention. These are some of the extra curriculum activities that I have been involved in and still am.

Chapter 21

Our Lives at Oadby, Leicestershire, 1984 onward.

L et me go back to 1984 when we moved to Oadby, Leicestershire. As mentioned previously, Church has always been the epicentre of our daily lives, so moving to Oadby Free Church was no exception. Oadby Church was similar to the one Brenda and I had been attending so far in Wolverhampton and Shrewsbury. So, moving to a different area meant that we had to find an alternative church, where we could settle down and make new friends. Our thoughts were that we should start with our nearest Evangelical Church and if we did not settle there for whatever reason, then we would move on to the next nearest one and so on. We were warmly welcomed at Oadby Evangelical Free Church, Oadby, and so there was no reason for us to look any further. We should bear in mind, that at any church, it is impossible to please everyone as we all have our different tastes, needs, cultural expectations and modes of music worship, etc. However, we settled there and became members of this church in 1984. Our main priority was for me to study and gain my professional qualifications in Social

Work as that was the main objective of our move to Leicester. Two years later, this goal had been accomplished and this was followed up by full-time employment in a local office situated in the Highfield area of Leicester. Therefore, this was another reason for us not to leave this area.

As time went on, Brenda and I became more and more involved in the life of the church. As we continued in our commitment, soon I was appointed as a Deacon with two other Church members, one of them being Norman H. It was a privilege to work with Norman. Both of us were later appointed as Elders at this Church. During our responsibilities, we formed strong bonds with each other and other Church Officers including our Minister at the time Michael S. It was such a joy to serve with each other in that capacity. Michael retired as the Minister of this church in September 2007 but he and his wife continue to attend the same church. Following Michael's retirement, I was then involved in the appointment of two consecutive Ministers, Adam B and Brandon N.

Regarding my siblings, after leaving home, there were never any relational difficulties and our bonds with each other became even stronger. These bonds continue to this day because we have stayed in touch with each other. As a wider family, we enjoy meeting together a couple of times a year. This includes all my brothers and sisters and their families. We call this a "Kalu Day". As we are now quite a large family we are mindful that not everyone can come every time, but those who can come, do. This keeps us together as a wider family.

Regarding my mother, whilst she was shopping in Wolverhampton, she had a heart attack and she was admitted to New Cross Hospital, Wolverhampton. My brother Satvant and I travelled to

Wolverhampton immediately and I spoke to the Consultant the following day and he confirmed that she was going to be fine. I stopped the night in Wolverhampton and visited her again the following day and late in the evening returned home. The following day Monday, as I was about to leave for work, I had a phone call from Newcross Hospital, Wolverhampton, saying that my mother was in a critical stage and we need to come immediately to the hospital. My brother Satvant and I left straight away to see her but she had passed away by the time we arrived. She passed away in March 1992.

Regarding my Dad, following my mother's death, my sister Jaswinder Kaur was still living at home and my brother Gurnam Singh lived nearby and between them, they did all the domestic care for him. My brother Satvant and I took turns to visit him every weekend and take him out for a drive and a snack. Eventually, he came to live in Oadby and his care was shared between Satvant's family and ours. He was so demanding and still wanting to be the head of our house. We could not do anything right for him. As we were out most of the day, we made arrangements for a carer to come in and prepare a meal and drinks for him. He was not happy with these arrangements. The carer left after several weeks. He would not let us appoint another one. On one occasion, he tried to make a cup of tea. He put the water into the electric kettle, a tea bag, sugar, and milk and switched on the kettle. All this resulted in no tea and the electric kettle being ruined and had to be replaced. When the children would return home from school, he would ask them, if they would like a cup of tea and follow on by saying, "mine is half a cup". He would say half a cup when he wanted a full cup. This is cultural. However, the children would only give him half a cup as he requested. Little did they realise that he wanted a full cup. On another occasion, I had brought some donuts for everyone, including him, to have after the main evening meal. As we were eating the main course, he suddenly grabbed the donut, dipped it in his gravy and ate it immediately. He thought he would not get one later on. The children were shocked that he dipped it in his gravy. They remember this to this day. Friday night was a Chinese takeaway and that was his highlight. We tried to make him as welcome as we could and integrate him into our family which was not easy. On one occasion, I especially went out of my way and cooked him some curry which I thought he would enjoy. The rest of the family was having a beef and kidney pie. He opted for the pie rather than the curry which I could not believe. He did not understand that we were both working full time and also looking after our children, foster children as well as him. He always wanted to be the centre of attention. Most evenings, he would have his evening meal and would then go straight to bed. Then he would be up in the middle of the night wandering about the house and talking to himself.

At that time, my work as a Principal Social Worker, for Northamptonshire was very demanding and involved a substantial amount of travelling across the country. As I was at work all day, daily life was becoming very stressful, as we were also fostering at the same time. He was beginning to show signs of dementia. He eventually went to live in a Residential Care Home, which was quite sad and eighteen months later he was admitted to the Leicester Royal Infirmary on 28th. August 1999. This was the day of our daughter Emma and Tim Couper's wedding day. I received a phone call from the Residential Care Home late evening. My brother Satvant and I visited him in the hospital twice but sadly, he died on 9th September 1999. Two days before this, a friend, Pastor Gurnam S, went to visit him in hospital. I understand from him that he gave his life to the Lord Jesus Christ and he became a Christian. This was wonderful news from our point of view. On the day he passed away, I was on my way to the hospital to visit him after work when I was informed that he had passed away that afternoon. I was so shocked, so I never saw him on that day. For the family's sake, he had a Sikh funeral at the Gurdwara and a Christian service at the Crematorium which was conducted by Pastor Gurnam.

Regarding our own immediate family, my wife and I enjoy our interaction and support with and from our immediate family. We now have ten grandchildren. They all look forward to seeing us and we love to see them. We have a very positive family environment because we all share the same values and long may it continue. Regarding Brenda's family, sadly Brenda's sister Melanie Oldacre passed away in September 2018. She is greatly missed by her family and by our wider family. We as a family keep in regular contact with them and visit them often. We also keep in touch with Brenda's other sister and her family. All of us meet whenever we can. Again it's a very positive environment when we meet. We are so grateful to have this relationship with them.

In 2008, our youngest daughter Lisa went to Jos, in Nigeria for two years, as a short termer with Serving in Mission, (SIM), organisation. She is a qualified teacher and her call was to work amongst the homeless, underprivileged children, and orphans. This was her ambition. Whilst she was serving in Nigeria, we had the opportunity to go and visit her for about two weeks, which we did. Visits such as this, make you aware and appreciate how fortunate we are to live in a country such as the United Kingdom. Here we all enjoy the facilities and the resources such as education and the NHS, etc. Countries such as Nigeria lack the majority of these resources as they are not organised in their infrastructure. Nigeria is not a poor country but many people live in poverty. The people live a chaotic lifestyle and live from one day to the other. Following our visit to see our daughter, we were challenged to consider, if we could help in one way or the other. Following lots of discussions, we made contact with SIM. Having done that, SIM discovered that there was a Special Educational Needs (SEN) school in Jos. This would be suitable for Brenda's placement as she is a qualified SEN teacher with several years of experience. Following several visits to the Nigerian Embassy in London, we were able to obtain a visa for our visit to Nigeria. During our stay in Nigeria, Brenda worked at the SEN school as well as with the orphaned children in various capacities. I was given the task of reviewing the orphanages and their child care services with City Ministries.

Within a few days of arriving in Jos, I was introduced to Peter (F) who was the Director of City Ministries and various other missionaries and local staff members, including some of the children. I was given free rein to talk to whoever I wanted to. This task also allowed me to visit several other orphanages run by City Ministries in other states. I got to know the work of City Ministries in depth. Having completed my findings, my report was well received and several recommendations were implemented. After this, we made several more visits doing voluntary work with the same organisation. We were planning to go back to Nigeria again in September 2014 but we were advised to go in January the following year as it was not safe to do so before that. Given that, we had planned to go in April 2015. This also had to be cancelled due to health reasons.

As time went by, in February 2015, as I was walking to church one Friday morning, I felt a little pain in my chest but was not sure what the cause of it was. The following Monday, Brenda and

I took two of our granddaughters on holiday to Wales. Whilst there, I went through the same symptoms again. It was at this stage, I thought that I ought to get myself medically checked out because Brenda and I were flying to Budapest a few days later. So the following morning, I got up early and told Brenda that I was going to the "Walk in Centre", in Oadby and that I will see her a bit later. On reaching the "Walk in Centre", I was eventually seen by a doctor who was not able to diagnose the problem. He asked if I wanted an angina spray or anti-acid tablets. I was told to have the ECG somewhere else. However, they agreed to give me a letter regarding the ECG, which I could take to the hospital. By now, Brenda had joined me and following discussion, we decided to go to the "Walk in Centre" at the Leicester Royal Infirmary. Having given the letter to the receptionist from the doctor, they agreed to do the ECG and within minutes it was done. From there on, I was immediately seen by the doctor who asked me numerous questions about my health and past family history and then told me to wait outside which I did. Within minutes a porter with a wheelchair arrived and asked me to sit on the wheelchair because I was being taken to the Accident and Emergency Department which was only a few yards away. I said to the porter, I am quite capable of walking there, but his response was, "you are not in a fit condition to walk, sir". I replied that I had walked two miles earlier this morning to the "Walk in Centre" so I should be able to walk to the A and E Department and again his response was the same. So, I quietly sat on the wheelchair and I was then wheeled to the A and E Department. Immediately on arrival, they started to attend to my health needs by taking a few samples of blood. Having done that, Brenda and I had to wait for the results to come and when they eventually did, I was informed that they want to do further tests. The next set of results would take a further two hours, I was told. I was feeling fine and energetic and could not understand what all the fuss was about. How can this be a heart problem? Unknown to Brenda and me, the doctor had already made arrangements for me to be admitted to Glenfield Hospital, Leicester for further tests. He then confirmed that I had had a heart attack and they wanted to do further tests and that arrangements had already been made for admission to Glenfield Hospital. I said in that case, we shall go home and pack few things together and will then make our way to Glenfield Hospital. His immediate response was no, saying that arrangements have already been made for me to be transferred by ambulance. At this stage, Brenda went home to gather few things together and I was taken to Glenfield Hospital by ambulance with a flashing blue light. As far as I was concerned, all this excitement and trauma was a waste of time and resources.

On arrival at Glenfield Hospital, the nursing staff were ready and waiting for me, and within minutes, I was being given further medication and injections and also, I was being wired up so that I could be monitored each moment of the day and night. Within a short time, I began to feel exhausted. I said to myself, "I was feeling OK until I came in here". I was not able to leave my bed area due to the fixed monitoring machine to the wall. That was the end of my freedom and independence so everything had to be brought to me. It became so difficult as members of the clinical staff were asking various questions, administering medication, checking for breathing, body temperature, heart rate, life history, taking blood, injections, and various other tasks. It certainly was not restful as this was happening night and day. I was being woken up in the middle of the night for observations. On the other hand, I had numerous family members and friends visiting whom I had not seen recently. So, it was good to catch up with them but I would have preferred this in better circumstances. I was feeling tired all the time and not being able to concentrate for a long period due to prescribed medication.

The following Friday, almost a week later, I was taken to the theatre for the angiogram procedure. I was feeling quite apprehensive but not too worried about the outcome. My view was that if there was a problem, which was unlikely, I would probably end up with one stent. At the end of the angiogram procedure, Sarah, the Consultant, came over and said, "Mr. Kalu, I am very, very sorry to tell you that you need a triple heart bypass." Two of your arteries are completely blocked and the third one is almost blocked". I was in total shock, which was not surprising. How could that be, I thought? I am not overweight, my BMI is fine, I eat healthily, I have never smoked or misused any drugs, and they are telling me that I need a triple heart bypass.

Having been in the recovery area for a very short time, I was taken on to the ward. I was feeling very low in mood. I eventually managed to phone Brenda and Lisa and asked them to come and they did immediately for which I was very grateful. I needed someone to talk to. I was in a state of unbelief. I was questioning my very thoughts about what I had just heard. Within five minutes of my arrival back on to the ward, there was the heart surgeon. It still had not sunk into my head the seriousness of the situation. However, I must stress that the nursing staff, including the consultants and doctors, were marvelous.

A few days later as I was going to the day room, I came across a lady who was in her mid-fifties. We had a brief conversation. She was also in the same predicament as I was. She told me that she was very scared of the operation and that she was having nightmares. She was restless and to cap it all, the following morning she had an appointment at her local dentist which she was dreading because she was having several of her teeth removed. No wonder she was in a state, firstly the dentist, then the related heart surgery. She said that she was feeling a little calmer having spoken to someone who understood the situation. We never saw each other again. My triple heart operation went ahead on the morning of 5th March 2015 and I was discharged from the hospital on 11th March 2015.

Coming back to my church life, I took three months off from my church duties and then resumed them again. I carried on as normal as I could but healing from an operation such as this takes a bit longer. However, life carried on as normal as possible.

Our Church Constitution states that Elders and Deacons can only be appointed for a term of six years, after which they can be reappointed by the church. There is also general guidance that officers should reconsider being reappointed on reaching the age of seventy years. As I only had sixteen months left before reaching this guidance age and my six years term of office was coming to an end, I had decided not to stand for re-election. I had served at OEFC as a Deacon and then as an Elder for twenty nine years. Just because you are no longer an officer within the church, it does not mean that you cannot continue to serve the Lord of your life. Brenda and I are still members at OEFC and we enjoy the fellowship there immensely. We are still involved in the life of this church and we will continue to do so for as long as we can. OEFC is part of our daily life.

Putting all these health issues aside, we had planned to return to Nigeria for another placement. We had placed the dates in our diaries to be in Jos from the beginning of January till Easter 2019. Having contacted SIM, they wanted an updated medical health report for our travel and the travel insurance. We made contact with our surgery for them to complete the paperwork three months before we were due to travel. Without the medical clearance, there was no point in booking the flights or applying for a visa. Our General Practice let us down immensely. Having made numerous visits to our surgery to check on the progress of this health report, even by the end of the year, they had not completed the forms. In the end, we had to abort our plans for our visit to Nigeria. Since then, we have not returned. Regardless of this, we are keeping in contact with some of the missionaries and the ongoing work. Nigeria is very much on our mind but there are other opportunities in which we are now involved.

Approximately ten years ago, I had the opportunity to visit a Christian Mission Station in Valathy, Tamil Nadu, India. It was a joint visit with another Pastor. This work was started by Ms. Betty Shelton, who was a missionary from Leicester. Since she started this Christian work, there are now over fifteen churches that have been planted and the work is progressing amidst severe opposition. In October 2019, Brenda and I had the privilege of visiting Valathy again. This was Brenda's first visit. It was such an uplifting experience. It was good to see the friends that I had made on my previous visit and to make new ones again. It was a tremendous visit and also an encouragement to those who are working there or associated with the work. If all goes well, we may make another visit in two or three years. We will have to wait and see. As part of this visit, my brother Satvant and I visited our family in Jandiala, near Jalandhar in Punjab. During our visit, we visited our auntie in Amritsar. It was good to go and see her again. This is the auntie I mentioned earlier in Part 1, who was married to my uncle Kehar Singh. Since our visit, she passed away in December 2019. I have very pleasant memories of spending time with her. Not only that, but we were also able to visit our maternal aunt and uncle, Shev Singh, and his wife Jito Kaur. We had not seen them for over forty years. They were both suffering from dementia and frailty and since our visit, they have also passed away. All I can say is that the effort to see them was worthwhile. They were so pleased to see us and remembered us well as youngsters.

Chapter 22

Reflective Thoughts and Hope for the Future

It's good to reflect on your life and think about your past experiences and possibly learn from them. Generally, life has been better than good. Sometimes, I think what life would have been if Dad had not come to England when he did. For him to come, great sacrifices had been made by Mum and Dad. Both of them being separated from each other for seven years and Mum trying to bring up the family alone. Dad not being able to see his children grow up and form a strong relationship with them. Hardships, which perhaps we never appreciated as youngsters because you are living in a different world. Hardships were also experienced by my maternal Grandparents who supported Dad financially which we were not aware of in our early days. We are forever thankful to them for the sacrifices they made, to give us the opportunity to be educated and to have a good standard of living as a family. Therefore, we shall be forever grateful to our parents. Also, we are grateful to our maternal grandparents, who supported Mum and us in the absence of Dad. It has not all been negative because we as children formed very strong bonds with them and this bond continues to this day with our cousins who are still in India. We visit them when we can and we have already introduced all our daughters and some grandchildren to them. This will continue as long as we can.

Dad became a Christian during the last couple of days of his life which gave him a new meaning in life. This decision gave him hope and life for the future. His decision also gives us hope as a family for the future. As Christians, we believe in life after death and when we leave this world, we shall meet him and greet him joyfully whatever, our differences had been in the past. This is something to look forward to in the future.

I mentioned at the beginning of Part 2, regarding the reservation some people had concerning our marriage. My wife and I are happy together and we have been married for forty-six years so far. We look forward to spending the rest of our future together.

We are thankful to our great God who has been guiding our lives. Without our Christian Faith, our lives would have been very different. Therefore, we enjoy living, seeing our families, our grandchildren, and our friends at the church. We can say with confidence that God has been our refuge and strength and our shining light. He has led us so far and He will continue to do so for the remainder of our lives. It is He who holds our future and we are confident that He will never let us down.

As I conclude, I would like to quote from the book that has been the foundation of our life and faith, the Bible.

For I am convinced that neither death nor life, neither angels nor demons, neither the present nor the future, nor any powers, neither height nor depth, nor anything else in all creation, will be able to separate us from the love of God that is in Christ Jesus our Lord.

Romans 8 v38 & 39

This is where our hope lies.

The End

Printed in the USA
CPSIA information can be obtained
at www.ICGtesting.com
LVHW020607111023
760703LV00010B/524

9 781838 496760